NAME:

wins ours

STUDY TOUR
READER

שְׁמַע יִשְׂרָאֵל יְהוָה אֱלֹהֵינוּ יְהוָה אֶחָד:

[בָּרוּךְ שֵׁם כְּבוֹד מַלְכוּתוֹ לְעוֹלָם וָעֶד]

וְאָהַבְתָּ אֵת יְהוָה אֱלֹהֶיךָ בְּכָל־לְבָבְךָ
וּבְכָל־נַפְשְׁךָ וּבְכָל־מְאֹדֶךָ:
וְהָיוּ הַדְּבָרִים הָאֵלֶּה אֲשֶׁר אָנֹכִימְצַוְּךָ הַיּוֹם עַל־לְבָבֶךָ:
וְשִׁנַּנְתָּם לְבָנֶיךָ וְדִבַּרְתָּ בָּם בְּשִׁבְתְּךָ
בְּבֵיתֶךָ וּבְלֶכְתְּךָ בַדֶּרֶךְ וּבְשָׁכְבְּךָ וּבְקוּמֶךָ:
וּקְשַׁרְתָּם לְאוֹת עַל־יָדֶךָ וְהָיוּ לְטֹטָפֹת בֵּין עֵינֶיךָ:
וּכְתַבְתָּם עַל־מְזֻזוֹת בֵּיתֶךָ וּבִשְׁעָרֶיךָ:

Shema Yisrael, Adonai Eloheinu, Adonai Echad.	**"Hear, O Israel: The Lord our God, the Lord is one!**
[Baruch sheim kvod malchuto l'olam vaed.]	[Blessed is the Name of His glorious kingdom forever and ever.]
V'ahavta eit Adonai Elohecha, B'chawl l'vav'cha, uv'chawl nafsh'cha, uv'chawl m'odecha.	You shall love the Lord your God with all your heart, with all your soul, and with all your strength.
V'hayu had'varim haeileh, Asher anochi m'tsav'cha hayom, al l'va-vecha.	And these words which I command you today shall be in your heart.
V'shinantam l'vanecha, v'dibarta bam b'shivt'cha b'veitecha, uvlecht'cha vaderech, uv'shawchb'cha uvkumecha.	You shall teach them diligently to your children, and shall talk of them when you sit in your house, when you walk by the way, when you lie down, and when you rise up.
Ukshartam l'ot al yadecha, v'hayu l'totafot bein einecha.	You shall bind them as a sign on your hand, and they shall be as frontlets between your eyes.
Uchtavtam, al m'zuzot beite-cha, uvisharecha.	You shall write them on the doorposts of your house and on your gates."

(Deuteronomy 6:4-9)

TABLE OF CONTENTS

Welcome to Twins Tours & Travel ltd

Twins Tours & Travel LTD is a Christian Arab agency specializing in building customized tour packages to the Holy Land, the birthplace of Judaism and Christianity. Our privilege as Israeli Arabs is having the opportunity to travel, not only in Israel but throughout the West Bank as well, and we look forward to sharing that with you. Experience the Bible's living history first-hand as you retrace the path of the Patriarchs and walk in the footsteps of Jesus. It is our aim that you and your fellow travelers will gain greater insight into the Scriptures as you connect with the land and the local Body of Christ. It has been both humbling, and a privilege to see numerous lives transformed as our groups experience the God of the Scripture personally through the intentional interaction with the Land of the Bible.

Mission Statement

To provide a journey of identity through learning the culture, the customs and the context of Scripture through Jesus' eyes, mind and heart.

Our Experience

In our experience of more than 20 years, most people leave this land changed forever. For those who have never been to Israel, it is hard to describe how much of a difference it makes to come and stand in the land of the Bible and see it for yourself. We have often heard it described as suddenly seeing in color after living in a world of black and white. There is no doubt that coming to the Holy Land will inject new life into the faith walk of tour participants with Jesus of Nazareth, and unveil a new appreciation for His Word.

In addition to offering Biblical study tours, we also offer a variety of tours, each with a different focus:

Biblical Study Tours

Faith Pilgrimages

Service/Volunteer Projects

Intercessory Prayer Journeys

Personally Customized/Specialized/Themed or Concept Tours

Conferences/Concerts

OUR VISION
Part of the vision of Twins Tours has always been to build up the local believing community by building bridges between Messianic Jews, Palestinian Christians, and the worldwide church. A service tour is an excellent opportunity for your group to take part in the day-to-day ministries of the 'living stones' of this land, and to experience first hand what God is doing today both in Israel and the Palestinian Territories.

THE LIVING STONES
Twins Tours specializes in ministry - church group tours. We are here to assist you in building a customized tour package that best suits your group type and budget. All of our guides are believers and fully licensed by the State of Israel, who are equally committed to providing your group with solid Biblical teachings as well as service and/or prayer opportunities during your trip to Israel.

TWINS TOURS TEAM
Twins Tours office staff look forward to meeting you and doing our best for your group to have the best experience in the Holy Land. We pray that while you are touring the land of the Bible you will have a special encounter with the Holy Spirit. We are so excited that you were able to make this trip of a lifetime!

Andre Moubarak: Owner & Manager / Main Guide

Tony Moubarak: Co-Manager / Main Guide

Marie Moubarak: Program Director & Resource Manager

Setrag Shemmessian: Tour Operator Manager

Sylvia Shemmessian: Accounting Manager

Sawsan Moubarak: Accounting Assistant

Albert Moubarak: Main communicator with guides and drivers.

Celesty Dabbagh: Media Projects Manager

TRIP LOG

DAY 1   DATE:

DAY 2   DATE:

DAY 3   DATE:

DAY 4   DATE:

DAY 5   DATE:

DAY 6   DATE:

DAY 7   DATE:

TRIP LOG

DAY 8   DATE:

DAY 9   DATE:

DAY 10   DATE:

DAY 11   DATE:

DAY 12   DATE:

DAY 13   DATE:

DAY 14   DATE:

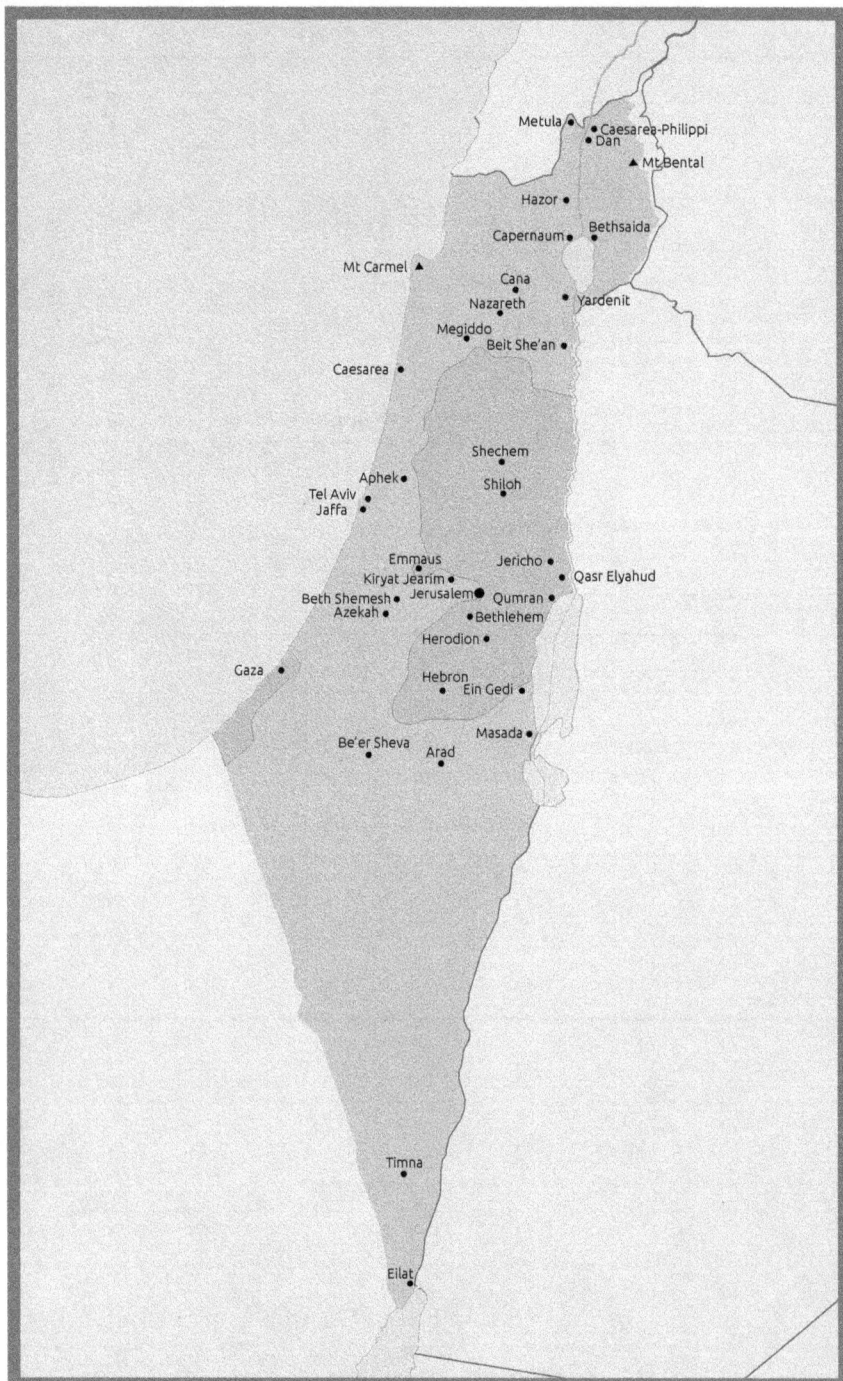

Metula •
• Caesarea-Philippi
• Dan
▲ Mt Bental

Hazor •

Capernaum • • Bethsaida

Mt Carmel ▲

Cana •
Nazareth • • Yardenit
Megiddo •
Beit She'an •

Caesarea •

Shechem •
Aphek • Shiloh •
Tel Aviv •
Jaffa •

Emmaus • Jericho •
Kiryat Jearim • • Qasr Elyahud
Beth Shemesh • Jerusalem • Qumran •
Azekah • • Bethlehem
Herodion •

Gaza •
Hebron •
• Ein Gedi

Be'er Sheva • Masada •
• Arad

Timna •

Eilat •

ANNUNCIATION CHURCH

DAY: **DATE:**   **TIME:**

Where the Word became Flesh!

The Church of the Annunciation in Nazareth sits on a site that is traditionally believed to have been the house of Mary; here, one can appreciate how Mary is revered by cultures all around the world. Underneath the church are ancient dwelling places, and nearby is a cemetery with a rolling stone from the 1st century AD *(Luke 1:26-38; John 1:14).*

ANTONIA FORTRESS

The Antonia Fortress was built by Herod the Great to overlook the Temple. It is believed that this was also the Praetorium where Pontius Pilate judged Jesus. This spot is therefore also the first station in the Via Dolorosa. Outside the fortress is the arch named Ecce Homo, Latin for "behold the man" *(John 18:28-19:16).*

DAY: **DATE:**   **TIME:**

Arad was a Canaanite stronghold whose king "fought against Israel and took of them prisoners" when they were trying to enter the promised land on more than one occasion. However, God delivered the Canaanites into the hands of Israel *(Num 21:1-3; 33:40; Judg 1:16)*.

AZEKAH

High above the valley of Elah was Azekah, the stronghold of the Kingdom of Judah. Azekah is the location where Joshua defeated the Amorite kings as the Lord destroyed them by a hailstorm. David fought Goliath in the valley below as the Israelites and Philistines camped on the hills. *(Josh 10:10-11; 1 Sam 17; Jer 34:7).*

BE'ER SHEVA

Be'er Sheva was an ancient Israelite fortified city located on the southern border of the land of Judah. The city is associated with Abraham and Isaac who gave it its name, meaning "Well of the Oath" or "Seven Wells" *(Gen 21:12-20,31-33; 22:19; 26:23-33; 28:10; 2 Sam 3:10; 1 Kgs 19:3-8)*.

BETHSAIDA

Bethsaida is a fishing village north of the Sea of Galilee, and is known as the birthplace of Peter, Andrew, and Philip. Jesus fed the 5000 in this area and healed a blind man here *(Mark 8:22-26; Luke 9:10-17; John 1:44).*

BEIT SHE'AN

This once-powerful city controlled the gateway to the land of Israel. On its walls, the Philistines hung the bodies of Saul and his three sons, whom they had defeated in battle on Mount Gilboa nearby *(1 Sam 31:8-12; 2 Sam 21:12; 1 Kgs 4:7,12)*.

The impressive remains seen today are from the Roman city, Scythopolis ("City of the Scythians") *(Col 3:11)*, built by Pompey as a capital city of the Decapolis where the Gospels say the fame of Jesus spread during his public ministry *(Matt 4:25; Mark 5:20; 7:31)*.

BOAT MUSEUM

The Ancient Galilee Boat, also known as the Jesus Boat, was found during a drought season, buried in the mud on the shore of the Sea of Galilee. This Roman boat was dated back to the time of Jesus and his disciples *(Matt 13:1-2; 14:22-33; Mark 4:35-41; Luke 5:1-11).*

BROAD WALL

DAY: **DATE:**   **TIME:**

Inside the Jewish Quarter, a section of the 8th century wall was uncovered. Hezekiah built this wall to defend Jerusalem against Sennacherib and the Assyrians after warnings from the prophet Isaiah. After the Jews returned in the time of Ezra and Nehemiah, they rebuilt the walls and re-established Temple worship *(2 Chr 32:1; Neh 4; Isa 22:10)*.

CAESAREA

Caesarea Maritima ("by the Sea") which is located on the Mediterranean coast, was one of the most important cities in the Roman world. The city was made great by none other than the visionary King Herod who built here a theater, hippodrome, aqueducts, and the world's largest artificial harbor. Cornelius, the God-fearing Gentile, calls for Peter to tell him the good news at Caesarea and there was baptized with the Holy Spirit *(Acts 10:1-8,24-28)*.

The Apostle Paul, accused of causing a riot, was sent to Caesarea to stand trial before the governor who resided there. As a prisoner, he shared his testimony in front of royalty and sailed to Rome to spread the message there as well *(Acts 23-26)*.

CAESAREA-PHILIPPI (BANIAS)

DAY: **DATE:**   **TIME:**

The Banias spring (named after the Greco-Roman god Pan) at
Caesarea Philippi is located at the foot of Mount Hermon and is one
of the main tributaries to the Jordan River. Here Jesus asked His
disciples, "who do men say that I am?". Simon (Peter) declares Jesus
to be the Messiah and Jesus renames him Peter saying, "on this rock
I will build my church" *(Matt 16:13-18; Mark 8:27-30; Luke 9:18-27)*. Up
the slopes of Mt Hermon is possibly the location of the magnificent
Transfiguration of Jesus *(Matt 17:1-13)*.

CAIAPHAS' HOUSE St Peter In Gallicantu

DAY: **DATE:**   **TIME:**

Located on the slopes on Mount Zion, this church is built on what is traditionally believed to be the house of the high priest Caiaphas. Jesus was brought here straight from the Garden of Gethsemane, where He faced the Sanhedrin before Pilate. Gallicantu, meaning "cock's crow," refers to Peter's triple denial of Christ in the courtyard of the house *(Matt 26:31-35; Luke 22:54-71).*

CANA

Cana is celebrated as the place where Jesus performed his first miracle, turning water into wine at a wedding *(John 2:1-11)*. The Wedding Church became a traditional place to perform weddings and to renew marriage vows.

CAPERNAUM

DAY: **DATE:**   **TIME:**

The fishing town of Capernaum became the hometown and headquarters of Jesus' ministry in Galilee *(Matt 4:13-16; 8:5-18; 17:24-27; Mark 1:21-38; 2:1-12; 9:33; Luke 4:23; John 4:46-52; 6:17,24,59).* Capernaum was also the home of Peter, the location of many miraculous healings, powerful teachings, and yet a town that Jesus eventually cursed for their unbelief *(Matt 11:23).* Capernaum sits on the border of two political territories, and at a tax station here, Jesus called Matthew, a tax collector, to be His disciple *(Mark 2:14).*

CHORAZIN

Chorazin / Korazim was one of the key towns in the Galilee where Jesus performed most of his miracles. However, it also became one of the cities Jesus denounced because of their lack of faith. *(Matt 11:20-24; Luke 10:13-16)*. The ruins of the town show houses made of basalt, as well as a synagogue with a "Moses Seat" *(Matt 23:1)*.

CITY OF DAVID

DAY: **DATE:**   **TIME:**

King David captured the small hilltop called Jerusalem from the
Jebusites and made it the unified capital of the new kingdom of
Israel. King Solomon later built the Temple to the north of the city
on the peak of Mount Moriah. The City of David, which included the
Temple Mount, grew and expanded over the years until it became
the Jerusalem we see today. *(Josh 15:63; 2 Sam 5:6-10; 2 Sam 24:16-25;
1 Kgs 6; 1 Chr 11:4-8; Matt 11:2-6; Heb 7:1-2).*

Hezekiah's Tunnel

DAY: **DATE:**   **TIME:**

In preparation for the siege by the Assyrians, King Hezekiah constructed a tunnel that would lead from the Gihon Spring to the Siloam (Shiloach) Pool to keep the water inside the city *(2 Kgs 20:20; 2 Chr 32:30)*.

Siloam Pool

DAY: **DATE:**   **TIME:**

A section of the ancient pool of Siloam/Shiloach, which was constructed in King Hezekiah's reign *(2 Kgs 20:20)*, was recently uncovered in the City of David. Jesus sends the man born blind to this pool after He heals him *(John 9)*.

DADO OBSERVATION POINT

DAY: **DATE:**   **TIME:**

The Dado observation point overlooks the border between Israel and Lebanon while giving a beautiful backdrop of Mt Hermon and the Hula Valley *(Ps 92:12; Song 4:15).*

METULA

DAY: **DATE:**   **TIME:**

Metula is the northernmost town in Israel with a viewpoint of the Lebanese border.

DAN

Tel Dan is a beautiful nature reserve with powerful springs that serve as the primary water source for the Jordan River. This site has unique remains of Canaanite and Israelite cities with a Biblical High Place and the replacement altar from Jeroboam's time *(Gen 14:14; Judges 18:29; 2 Sam 3:10; 1 Kgs 12:29-30)*.

The most unique finding is the Tel Dan Stele, which is a broken stone with an inscription mentioning "House of David." It is considered the earliest mention of David outside the Biblical sources.

DAY: **DATE:**   **TIME:**

The Davidson Center is a museum and archeological park where one can go back in time and walk along the 2,000 year old road and see the remains of arches and huge stones that fell from the walls of the original Temple Mount. Next to the Southern Wall, one could climb up the staircase carved into the bedrock of Mount Moriah which lead up to the Temple through the Hulda Gates *(Matt 4:5; 12:6; 21:12-16; 24:1-2; Mark 11:27).*

DEAD SEA

The Dead Sea, also known as the Salt Sea *(Gen 14:3),* is located on the border between Israel and Jordan and happens to be the lowest place on earth, with shores near 430 meters below sea level. This lake is also one of the saltiest bodies of water in the world. With 35% salinity, it makes it difficult for any life to exist in the lake but allows for a relaxing float in its mineral-rich waters *(Ezek 47:8-12).*

DOMINUS FLEVIT

DAY: **DATE:**   **TIME:**

The Dominus Flevit, which means "the Lord has wept," is a church located on the foothills of the Mount of Olives. When Jesus came from Bethany and rode on the donkey down to Jerusalem, He visualized its destruction and wept over it *(Luke 19:41)*.

Ein Gedi

Ein Gedi is the largest oasis on the western shore of the Dead Sea. Its freshwater springs allow for beautiful vegetation (such as palm trees and vineyards), as well as animal life (such as the ibex and hyrax) to thrive *(Song 1:14; Ps 104:18)*. Ein Gedi also served as a place of refuge for David when he was fleeing from Saul *(1 Sam 24; Ps 57)*.

EIN KAREM

Ein Kerem, the picturesque village full of winding lanes, luscious green gardens, and enchanting architectural features, is traditionally accepted as the "town in the hill country of Judea" where John the Baptist was born *(Luke 1)*.

DAY: **DATE:**   **TIME:**

The valley of Elah is a corridor connecting the coastal cities with the inland cities like Jerusalem and Bethlehem and the location of the famous battle between David and Goliath *(1 Sam 17)*.

GARDEN TOMB

DAY: **DATE:**   **TIME:**

The Garden Tomb is believed by many to be the location of the burial and resurrection of Jesus *(Matt 27:57-60; John 19:41)*. The beautiful and tranquil garden with the rock-cut tomb became a center for Christian worship and contemplation.

DAY: **DATE:**   **TIME:**

The Church of the Agony and the Garden of Gethsemane, located at the foot of Mount of Olives, commemorate Jesus' last night before he was delivered into the hands of those who would crucify him. *(Matt 26:36; Mark 14:32)*. In the garden, Jesus' despair was so deep that he sweated drops of blood *(Luke 22:43-44)*.

HERODION

Located near Jerusalem and Bethlehem, this fortress was built by none other than King Herod, the "builder-king" *(Matt 2:1-22)*. In this ambitious project, he raised the mountain up to further protect the splendid palace which served as a summer home. King Herod also built a monumental tomb for himself on the slopes of the hill facing Jerusalem. The site was later used by Jews during the great revolts against the Romans.

HOLY SEPULCHRE CHURCH

DAY: **DATE:**   **TIME:**

The Church of the Holy Sepulchre has been continuously recognized since the 4th century as the site of Jesus' death, burial, and resurrection *(Matt 27:33-28:10; Mark 15:21-16:8; Luke 23:26-24:10; John 19:16-20:18)!*

Hula Valley

The Hula Lake was located in the Jordan Valley, about 10 miles north of the Sea of Galilee. It may have been the "Merom Waters" where Joshua met the 5 kings in battle (Josh 11:5-7). Since the establishment of the State of Israel, the lake (or rather, the swamp) had been drained and later reflooded to serve different agriculture and ecological purposes.

Israel is a blessed land bridge for God''s creatures and this swamp today is a resting point for millions of birds in their annual migration between Europe, Asia, and Africa — making the Hula Valley one of the best spots in the world for birdwatching.

JAFFA / TEL AVIV

DAY: **DATE:**   **TIME:**

Jaffa (Joppa) is one of the oldest port cities in Israel and the Mediterranean. In an attempt to flee from the presence of God, Jonah came to Jaffa port to find a ship sailing to Tarshish *(Jonah 1:3)*. Peter the apostle was staying at Simon the Tanner's house, in Jaffa, when he received the vision that started his ministry to the Gentiles *(Acts 10; 11:5)*.

JERICHO

Jericho, the "City of Palms" *(Judg 3:13)* is located at the northern end of the Dead Sea and is the oldest walled city in the world, first inhabited over 9000 years ago. It was conquered by resounding trumpets as Joshua led the Israelites around the heavily fortified walls of Jericho *(Josh 6)*. Nearby is the view of the monastery on Mt. Qarantal (Mount of Temptation) commemorating Jesus' 40 days in the wilderness *(Matt 4:1-11; Mark 1:12,13)*.

The gospels share records of Jesus healing two blind men at Jericho *(Matt 20:29-34; Luke 18:35-43)*, and there he also met with Zaccheus — the tax collector who was up in a sycamore tree *(Luke 19:1-10)*.

JORDAN RIVER

From crossing the river into the Promised Land to being baptized in its waters, the Jordan River represents a physical and spiritual boundary throughout the scriptures *(Gen 13:10; Num 32; Deut 3; Josh 3-4; 2 Sam 19; 2 Kgs 2; Matt 3; Mark 1; Luke 3; John 1).*

MIGDAL (MAGDALA)

DAY: **DATE:**   **TIME:**

Magdala, the home of Mary Magdalene, was a major port village on the shore of the Sea of Galilee and a center for trade and commerce. A 1st century synagogue was uncovered here; it is believed to have been used frequently by Jesus as he taught in the Galilee region *(Matt 4:23)*.

MASADA

Masada (Hebrew for "fortress") is a spectacular ancient fortress in the Judean Desert. It was built by Herod the Great on top of a steep and isolated hill which overlooks the Dead Sea. Masada was the last and most important Jewish stronghold to fall captive to the Romans in the Great Revolt (66-73 AD) *(1 Sam 22:3-5; 23:14; 24:22; Ps 18:2; 71:3; Isa 33:14-16)*.

DAY: **DATE:**   **TIME:**

Megiddo was a strategic site located on the crossroads of ancient trade routes and currently sits on 27 layers of ruins. Many pharaohs, kings, and emperors fought bloody battles in the Jezreel Valley to control this strategic pass. No wonder this is said to be the location of the final battle of Armageddon *(Rev 16:16)*.

DAY: **DATE:**   **TIME:**

Mount Arbel is a striking cliff in the eastern lower Galilee overlooking the lake. Brutal battles took place here, such as when the Jews fought against Herod for control of the Galilee *(2 Kgs 17:3; Hos 10:14)*.

The passageway below was part of the ancient route called the Via Maris. Jesus would have traveled this route as he went through the different Galilee villages *(Matt 9:35)*.

DAY: **DATE:**   **TIME:**

Overlooking the north-vwestern shore of the Sea of Galilee, Mount of Beatitudes is believed to be the setting where Jesus taught about the Kingdom of Heaven in the "Sermon on the Mount" *(Matt 5-7)*.

MOUNT BENTAL

DAY: DATE: TIME:

Mount Bental is a dormant volcano in the Golan Heights overlooking the borders with Syria *(Matt 4:24)*.

MOUNT CARMEL

DAY: **DATE:** **TIME:**

Starting at Haifa and stretching south-east from the Mediterranean Sea, this coastal range has been considered a sacred place throughout history because of its beauty and fertility. It was on Mount Carmel that Elijah challenged the 450 prophets of Baal to see who is the real God *(1 Kings 18:16-40)*.

MOUNT OF OLIVES

DAY: **DATE:**   **TIME:**

The Mount of Olives is a three-summit mountain ridge east of the Old City in Jerusalem. Jesus raised Lazarus from the dead in Bethany, which is located on this hill *(John 11:1-44)*. Nearby, in the village of Bethphage, the disciples found the donkey and colt which Jesus rode on his entry to Jerusalem on Palm Sunday *(Zech 9:9; Matt 21:1-11)*.

Jesus ascended to heaven from the Mount of Olives with a promise of sending the Holy Spirit (Acts 1:1-12) and to this mountain He will one day return (Zech 14:4)!

MOUNT PRECIPICE

DAY: **DATE:**   **TIME:**

Just south of Nazareth is the cliff of Mount Precipice. It is traditionally
believed to have been the spot where the mob attempted to throw
Jesus off the cliff after he proclaimed the fulfilled prophecy at
the synagogue in Nazareth. Also known as the Mount of the Leap
(Luke 4:16-30).

NATIVITY CHURCH

The Church of the Nativity in Bethlehem is the oldest church in the world, built by Roman Emperor Constantine's mother Queen Helena in the 4th c AD. It was built over a humble cave venerated as Christ's birthplace. "And [Mary] brought forth her firstborn Son, and wrapped Him in swaddling cloths, and laid Him in a manger, because there was no room for them in the inn." *(Luke 2:7)* And thus was fulfilled the prophecy that the Messiah would be born in Bethlehem *(Mic 5:2)*.

DAY: **DATE:**   **TIME:**

Nazareth Village is a delightful re-creation of the Galilean Jewish village in the time of Jesus. This open air museum re-enacts the village life while illustrating different Biblical parables *(Matt 2:23; Luke 2:39-40, 4:16)*.

Pools of Bethesda

DAY: DATE: TIME:

In Jerusalem near one of the gates, were the legendary healing pools of Bethesda. Many came to be healed, but Jesus went to one man who was had a disability for 38 years. "Pick up your mat and walk!" He said, and the man was instantly healed *(John 5:2-18)*!

QASR EL YAHUD

The traditional site on the Jordan River where Jesus was baptized by John the Baptist in preparation for his ministry *(Matt 3:13-17; Mark 1:9-11; Luke 3:21-22; John 1:28-34)*. Coincidentally, it is also believed to be the location where the children of Israel crossed over into the promised land with Joshua, carrying the ark of the covenant *(Josh 3:15-17)*, also where, 300 years later, the prophet Elijah was taken to heaven on chariots of fire *(2 Kgs 2:7-14)* - adding to the significance of John baptizing here in the spirit and power of the prophet Elijah *(Luke 1:15-17)*.

Another possible location is "Bethany Beyond the Jordan" (Al-Maghtas in Arabic) which is located on the eastern side of the Jordan River *(John 1:28; 10:40)*.

QUMRAN

DAY: **DATE:**   **TIME:**

Located on the north-western shore of the Dead Sea, the site of Qumran is most famous for the Dead Sea Scrolls that were found in its caves in the 1940s and 50s. Fragments of almost all the books of the Old Testament were found, dating back to the 3rd century BC. Though these scrolls are 1,000 years older than other Hebrew manuscripts, there are very few differences, indicating the miracle of God's protection of His Word throughout history. It is possible that John the Baptist was part of the community living in Qumran (Isa 40:3; Mark 1:6).

SEA OF GALILEE

Also known as the Kinneret or Lake Tiberias, the Sea of Galilee is a freshwater lake in northern Israel. It is located in the Jordan Valley with the Jordan River passing right through it till it reaches the Dead Sea. The Sea of Galilee allowed for thriving fishing villages to form around it, becoming a primary scene for Jesus' ministry, whether on the lake itself or around it *(Isa 9:1-2; Mark 6:45-56; Luke 5:1-11; John 6).*

SHEPHERD'S FIELD

DAY: **DATE:**   **TIME:**

In the area east of Bethlehem is the Shepherd's Field Church, which, as the name suggests, is where the angel of the Lord appeared and proclaimed the birth of the Messiah to the shepherds. "Glory to God in the highest, and on earth peace, goodwill toward men!" *(Luke 2:8-20).*

DAY: **DATE:**   **TIME:**

At the foot of Mount Beatitudes are the two churches of Tabgha. The Church of the Multiplication of the Loaves and Fishes *(Mark 6:30-44; John 6:1-14),* which remembers the miracle of Jesus feeding the 5,000, and the Church of the Primacy of St Peter. Being a favorite fishing spot, it is believed that Jesus called his first disciples on these shores *(Mark 1:16-20; Luke 5:1-11).* After Jesus' resurrection, he appeared, for the third time, to his disciples here and had lunch with them. The church commemorates Jesus affirming and restoring Peter as he commissioned him to feed His sheep *(John 21:1-19).*

TEMPLE INSTITUTE

This museum illustrates the evolution of Jewish worship from the Tabernacle in the wilderness to Solomon's Temple, Nehemiah & Ezra's Temple, and Herod's Temple at the time of Jesus. The plans for building the 3rd Temple in the future can also be seen.

TEMPLE MOUNT

The Temple Mount is inside the Old City and north of the City of David. There were three stages (or two and a half) of the Temple, built by King Solomon, Zerubbabel, and King Herod (who renovated the one Zerubbabel made). Jesus preached at the Temple many times as it was the center for prayer and worship. It was destroyed by the Romans in 70 AD and later replaced by Muslim shrines. *(Gen 22:1-18; 2 Sam 24:16-25; 1 Kgs 6; 1 Chr 21:14-22:1; 2 Chr 3:1; Ezra 3:8, 4:3). (Matt 21:12-15,23; 27:5-6; Mark 12:35-44; Luke 1:9,21-23; 2:27,37,46; 19:47; John 2:14-21; 10:23; Acts 2:46; 3:2-11; 5:20-25,42; 17:24).*

VIA DOLOROSA

DAY: **DATE:**   **TIME:**

The Via Dolorosa, also known as the Way of the Cross, is a processional route in the Old City of Jerusalem. It consists of 14 stations in which one can identify with the suffering of Jesus all the way from the place of judgment by Antonia Fortress, continuing west to the Holy Sepulchre Church where He was crucified and buried *(Matt 27:25; Mark 15:16-25; Luke 23:26-34)*.

WESTERN WALL

The Western Wall, also known as the Wailing Wall, is a remnant of the retaining wall for the grand Temple built by King Herod. It is believed to be the clostest part to the Holy of Holies. The Western Wall is the holiest place in the world for the Jewish people. Along the Western Wall are underground tunnels that connect the western wall prayer area to the Via Dolorosa *(1 Kings 6; 8:41-42).*

YARDENIT

Yardenit ("little Jordan") is a popular baptism site situated where the Sea of Galilee feeds into the Jordan River — just before it meanders south through the Jordan Valley *(Matt 28:19-20; Mark 1:4-5; Luke 3:21-22; 3:16; Acts 2:38-41; 8:36-38; 10:48; 16:31-33; 22:16; Col 2:12).*

YAD VASHEM

Located in Jerusalem, Yad Vashem, meaning "a hand and a name" *(Isa 56:5)* is Israel's official memorial museum for the victims of the Holocaust.

APHEK

Overlooking an international highway, Aphek, also known as Antipatris, has always been a strategic fortress. At one point, it was the location of the Philistine encampment at the Battle of Ebeneaser where the Ark of the Covenant was captured (*1 Sam 4:1-11; 29:1; 1 Kgs 20:26-30*). After Paul's arrest in Jerusalem, the Romans took him to Caesarea to protect him from those after his life, and they rested at Antipatris which was halfway between Jerusalem and Caesarea (*Acts 23:23-35*).

BETH SHEMESH

Beth Shemesh ("House of the Sun") was an important Biblical city on the border between the Israelites, Canaanites, and Philistines. When the ark of the covenant was taken by the Philistines after the battle of Ebenezer, they sent it back on two cows to Beth Shemesh (*1 Sam 6:10-21*). This is also the location of the battle between King Amaziah of Judah and King Jehoash of Israel after the kingdom split (*2 Kgs 14:11-14*). Samson's stories took place in the Sorek valley region where Beth Shemesh is located (*Judg 13-16*).

EILAT

The southern city of Israel on the tip of the Red Sea. Eilat, being a border city, was a sea port built by King Solomon (*1 Kgs 9-10; 22; 2 Kgs 14:22*). Further south beyond the Israeli border was one of the wilderness stops where the children of Israel stayed before entering the Promised Land. Some of the world's most beautiful coral reefs are found in the Red Sea.

EMMAUS (ROAD TO)

Two disciples were walking along the road from Jerusalem to Emmaus on the day of the resurrection. While still downcast over the events of Jesus' death and confused about the rumors of the empty tomb, Jesus joined them in disguise and explained all the scriptures concerning himself. After having dinner with them, their eyes were open. Jesus vanished, but they ran all the way back to Jerusalem to let the other disciples know that Jesus is indeed alive (*Luke 24:13-35*)!

HAZOR

Hazor was an important major city mentioned in Joshua as "the head of all those kingdoms" (*Josh 11:10-13*). Jabin, the Canaanite king of Hazor, sent his commander Sisera to fight Barak, but he was killed, and later Jabin defeated as well (*Judg 4*). King Solomon rebuilt the city, and later King Ahad expanded it (*1 Kgs 9:15*). The city today is the largest tel in Israel (about 200 acres).

HEBRON

Hebron, which means "friend" (*Isa 41:8*), is the ancient site by the "terebinths of Mamre," where Abraham and his family lived. Abraham, Sarah, Isaac, Rebecca, Jacob, and Leah were buried in the Machpelah cave - the Cave of the Patriarchs (*Gen 13:18; 23:19; 37:14; 49:29-32*). When David first became king, he ruled Hebron for seven and a half years before establishing his rule in Jerusalem (*1 Sam 30:31; 2 Sam 2:1; 5:3-5; 1 Kgs 2:11*).

KIRYAT JEARIM

After the Philistines returned the Ark of the Covenant to Beit Shemesh, it was brought to Kiriyath Jearim to the house of Aminadab. King David later brought it into Jerusalem with music and dancing (*1 Sam 6:21-7:2; 2 Sam 6*).

SHECHEM (NABLUS)

Located in the hills of Samaria, between Mount Gerizim and Mount Ebal, Shechem is the place where Abraham first received the promise of the land being given to his descendants. Jacob buys land at Shechem and his sons were tending the sheep here when Joseph is sent to find them (*Gen 12:6; 33:18; 35:4; 37; Josh 21:21; 24:1, 25, 32; Judg 9; 1 Kgs 12:1; Ps 60:6; Jer 41:5*).

SHILOH

Shiloh, located in the hills of Samaria, was the ancient assembly and worship center where the Tabernacle stood during the times of the Judges. The young prophet Samuel was raised here until the Ark of the Lord was taken at the Battle of Ebenezer. Shiloh was destroyed, but Samuel led the people until it came time to set a king over Israel (*Josh 18:8-10; Judg 21:19; 1 Sam 1-4; Ps 78:59-64,70-72*).

TIMNA

Located south of Israel is the large nature and historical park of Timna which is full of beautiful geological formations. This valley was used for copper mining during Biblical times (*Deut 8:9; Job 28:2; Ezek 22:20; Luke 21:2*). The highlight of Timna though, is the life-size model of the Tabernacle in the wilderness (*Exod 25:1-9*).

GEOGRAPHICAL REGIONS

The Coastal Plain - the flat coastal region running along the Mediterranean Sea from Rosh Hanikra to the Gaza Strip. Most of Israel's population lives here.

The Hill Country - Also known as the Judean or Central Mountains it is a region consisting of three mountain ranges: Hebron in the south, Judea in the center, and Samaria in the north.

The Jordan Valley - The Jordan Valley is the geographic and political dividing line between Israel in the west and Jordan to the east. It was created as a result of the Syrian-African rift which created the lowest elongated crack in the earth's crust. The Jordan Valley today includes the Hula Valley, the Sea of Galilee, the Jordan River, the Dead Sea and down the Aravah Valley to the Gulf of Aqaba at the Red Sea.

The Negev - the beautiful Negev Desert covers over half of Israel's total land area with less than 10% of its population.

"But the land you are crossing the Jordan to take possession of is a land of mountains and valleys that drinks rain from heaven. It is a land the Lord your God cares for; the eyes of the Lord your God are continually on it from the beginning of the year to its end."

(Deut 11:11-12)

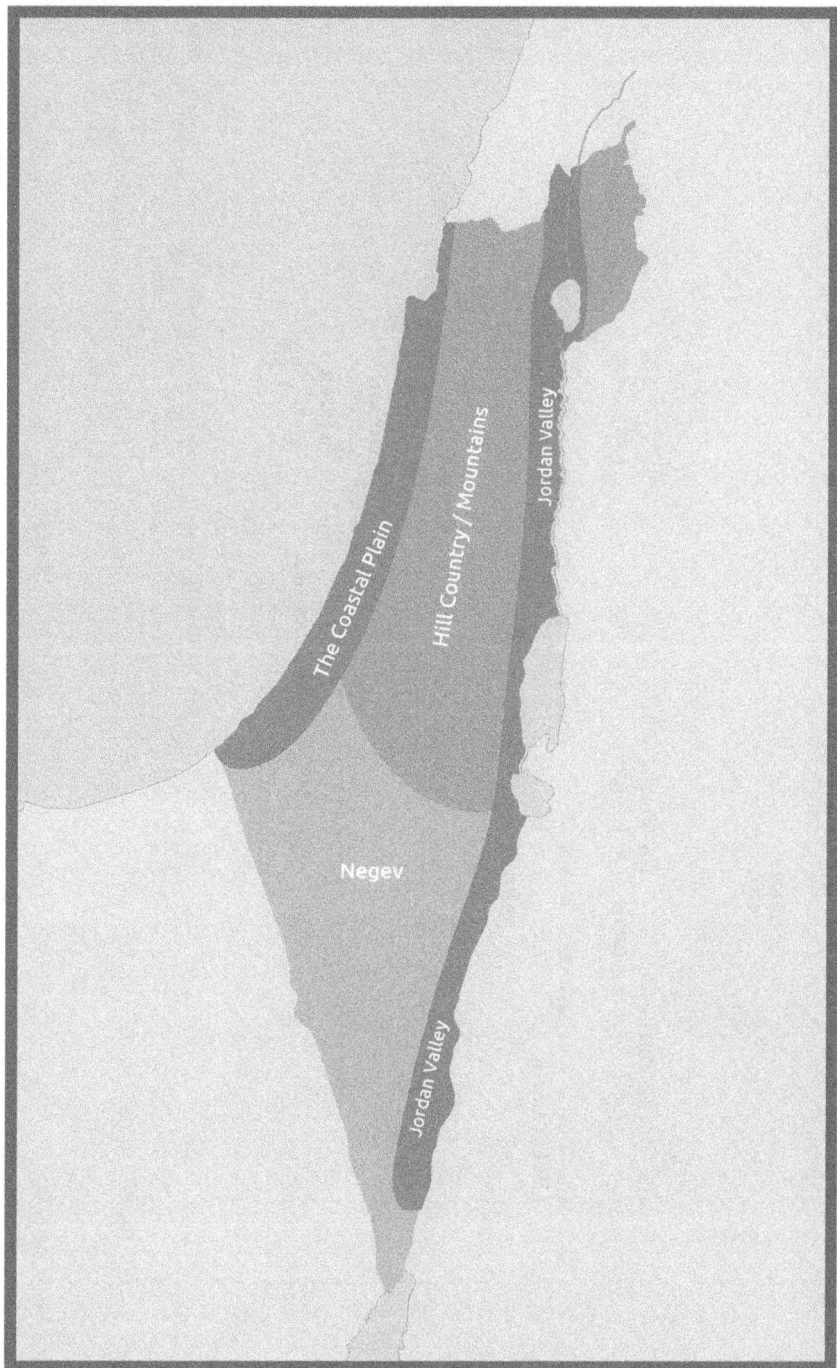

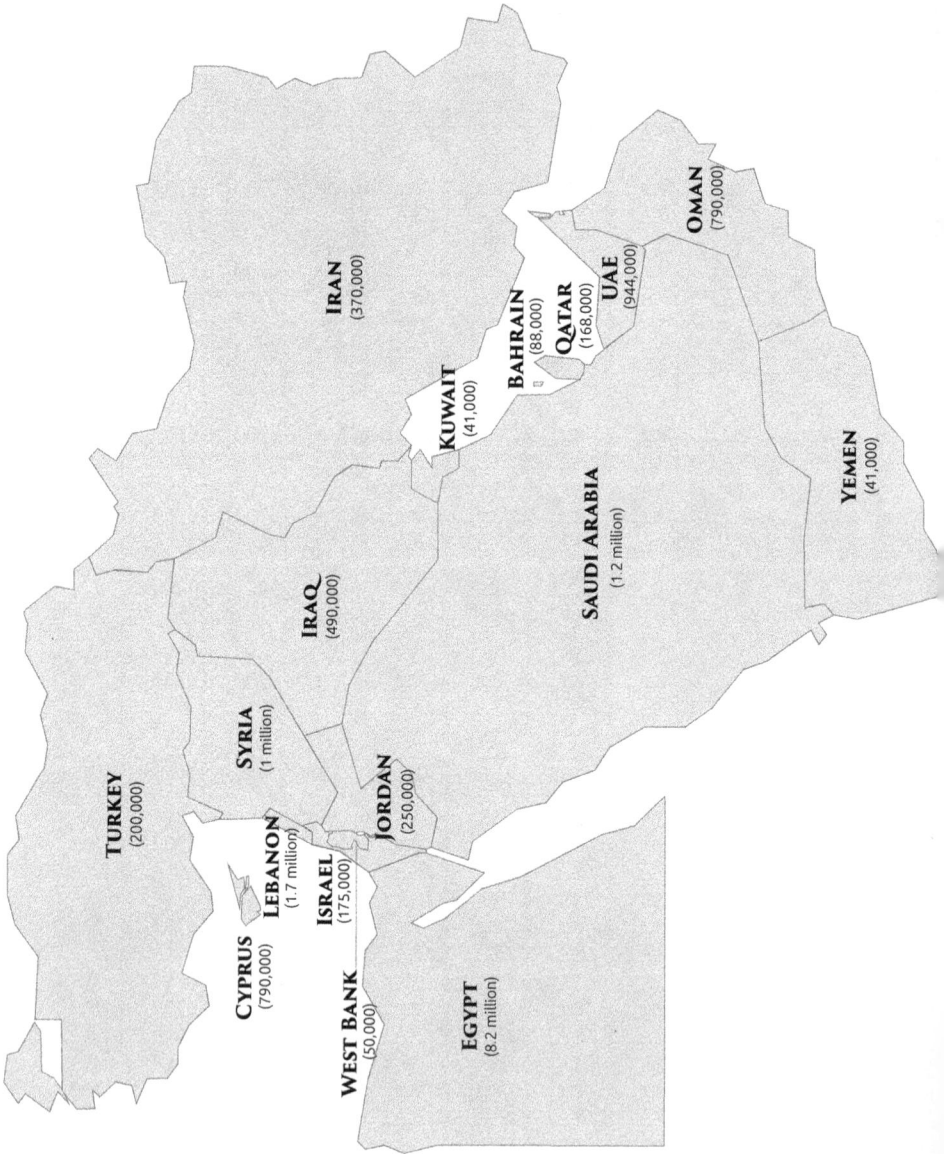

OMAN
(790,000)

IRAN
(370,000)

UAE
(944,000)

QATAR
(168,000)

BAHRAIN
(88,000)

KUWAIT
(41,000)

YEMEN
(41,000)

SAUDI ARABIA
(1.2 million)

IRAQ
(490,000)

SYRIA
(1 million)

JORDAN
(250,000)

TURKEY
(200,000)

LEBANON
(1.7 million)

ISRAEL
(175,000)

CYPRUS
(790,000)

WEST BANK
(50,000)

EGYPT
(8.2 million)

CHRISTIANS IN ISRAEL (10 FACTS)

1. Christians in Holy Land are a very small minority group of 175,000, comprising 2 percent of the population.

2. Christmas is a regular workday in Israel. Banks, government offices, stores are all open.

3. Most Holy Land Christians, 80%, are indigenous Arabs.

4. Around 70% of Christians live in northern Israel. The largest number of the Christian Arab community, is in Nazareth (22,100), the second largest is in Haifa (15,000), and third largest in Jerusalem (12,600).

5. The median marriage age for a Christian groom is 29 and 25 for a bride.

6. Christian families usually have only one to two children.

7. Christian women are more educated than their peers, with 75% studying toward a second degree.

8. Israeli Christians belong primarily to four denominations; Greek-Orthodox, Non-Chalcedonian Orthodox, Roman Catholic and few Protestant (1% of the 2% in Israel).

9. The Most significant Christian site is the Church of the Holy Sepulchre, placed at the site of Jesus' crucifixion in the fourth century.

10. The largest church in the Middle East is the Church of the Annunciation, located in Nazareth.

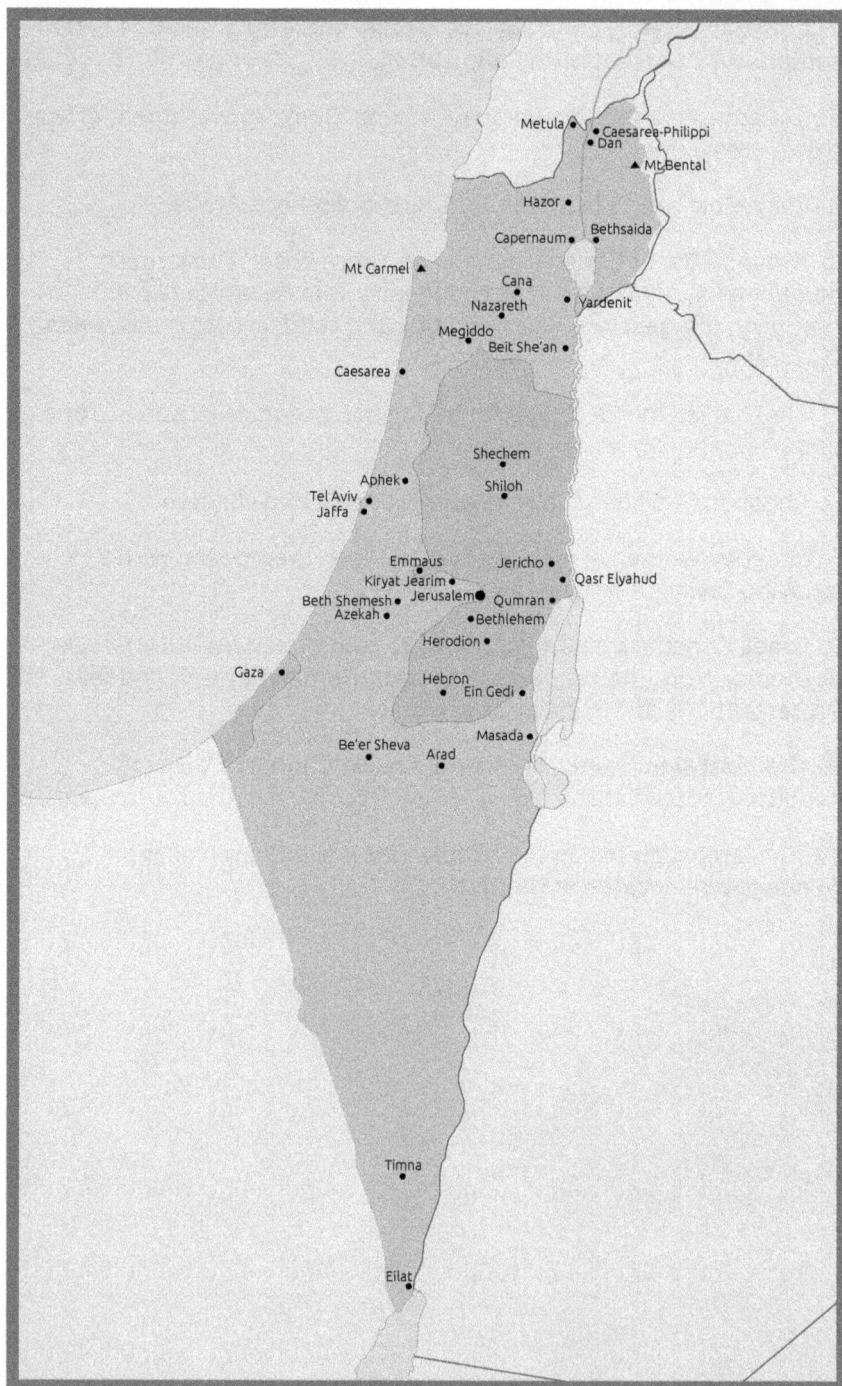

Metula
Caesarea-Philippi
Dan
Mt Bental
Hazor
Capernaum
Bethsaida
Mt Carmel
Cana
Nazareth
Yardenit
Megiddo
Beit She'an
Caesarea
Shechem
Aphek
Shiloh
Tel Aviv
Jaffa
Emmaus
Jericho
Kiryat Jearim
Qasr Elyahud
Beth Shemesh
Jerusalem
Qumran
Azekah
Bethlehem
Herodion
Gaza
Hebron
Ein Gedi
Masada
Be'er Sheva
Arad
Timna
Eilat

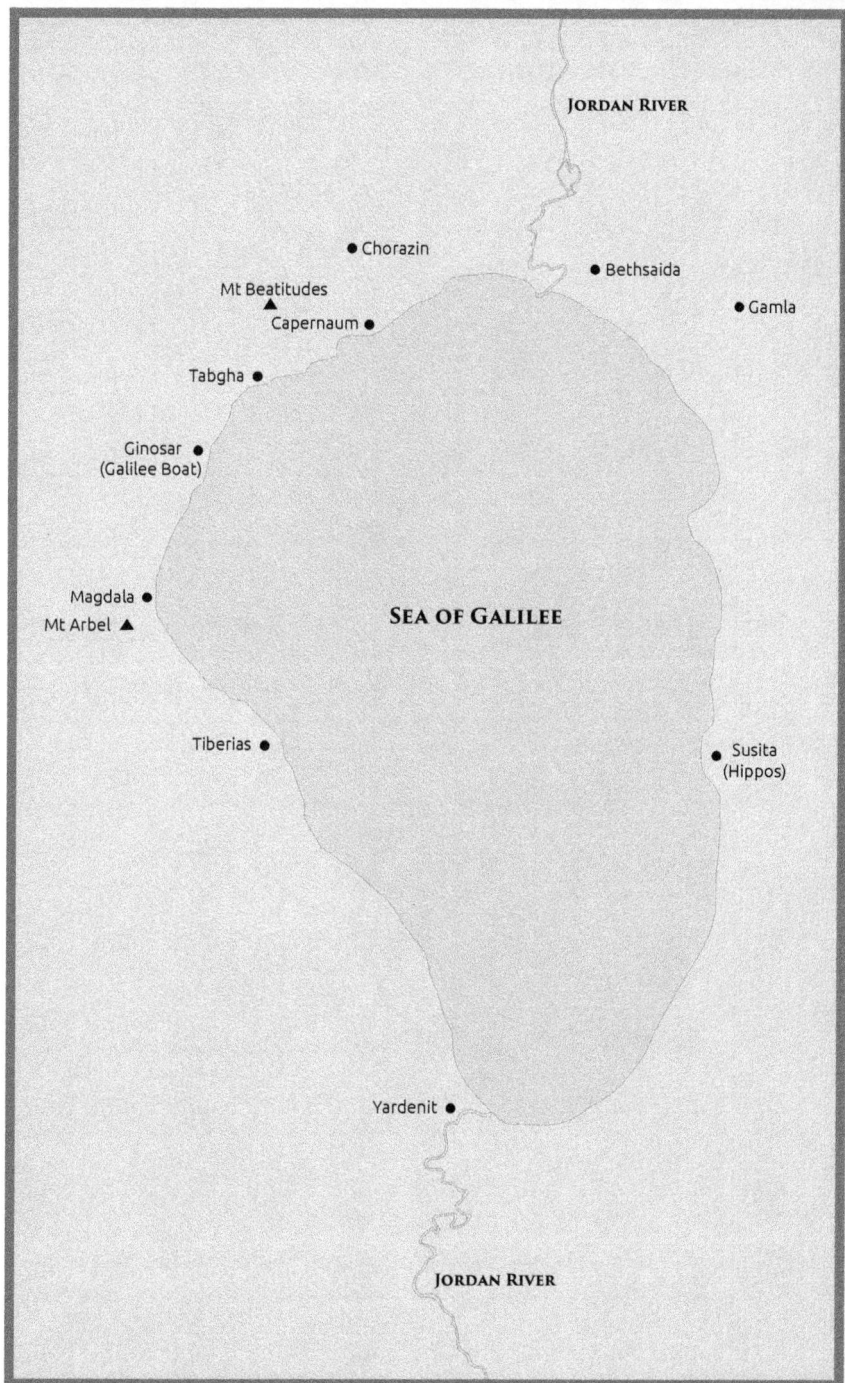

JORDAN RIVER

● Chorazin

● Bethsaida

Mt Beatitudes ▲

● Gamla

Capernaum ●

Tabgha ●

Ginosar ●
(Galilee Boat)

SEA OF GALILEE

Magdala ●
Mt Arbel ▲

Tiberias ●

● Susita
(Hippos)

Yardenit ●

JORDAN RIVER

125

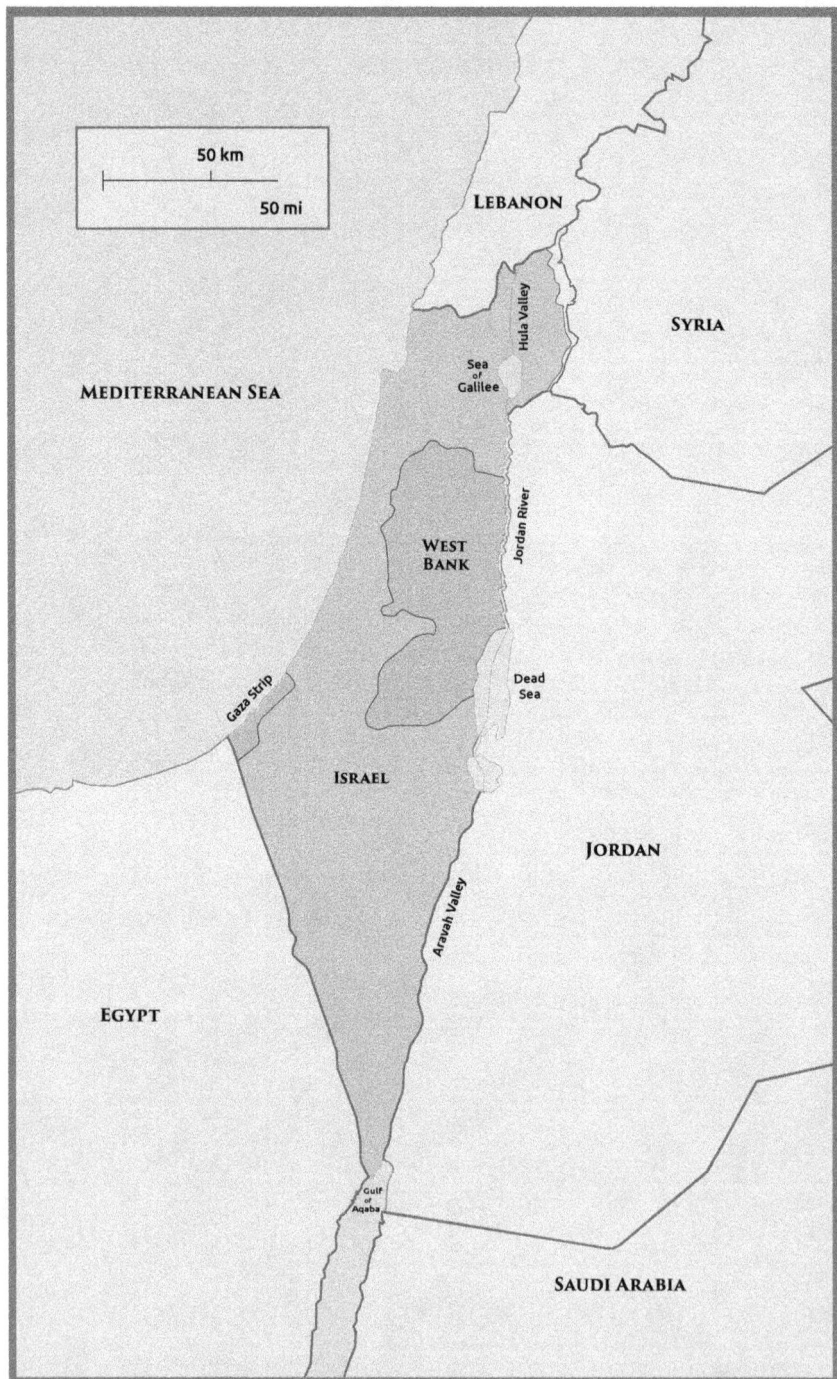

50 km

50 mi

LEBANON

SYRIA

Hula Valley

Sea of Galilee

MEDITERRANEAN SEA

Jordan River

WEST BANK

Gaza Strip

Dead Sea

ISRAEL

JORDAN

Aravah Valley

EGYPT

Gulf of Aqaba

SAUDI ARABIA

THE WEST BANK

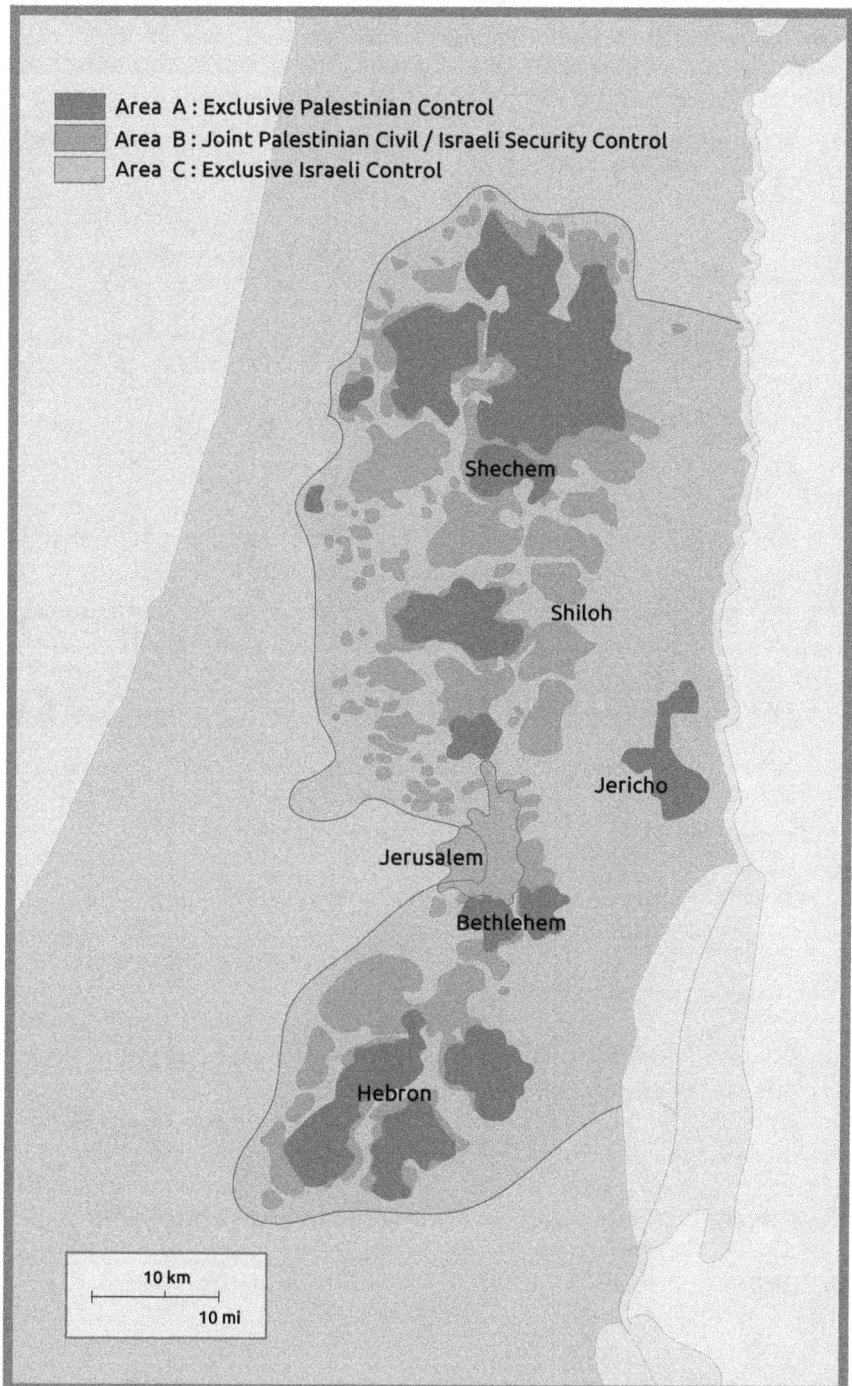

Area A : Exclusive Palestinian Control
Area B : Joint Palestinian Civil / Israeli Security Control
Area C : Exclusive Israeli Control

Shechem

Shiloh

Jericho

Jerusalem

Bethlehem

Hebron

10 km
10 mi

Jerusalem on Madaba Map

The Madaba Map is a floor mosaic in the Church of Saint George in Madaba, Jordan. Part of this map contains the oldest cartographic depiction of the Holy Land and especially Jerusalem.

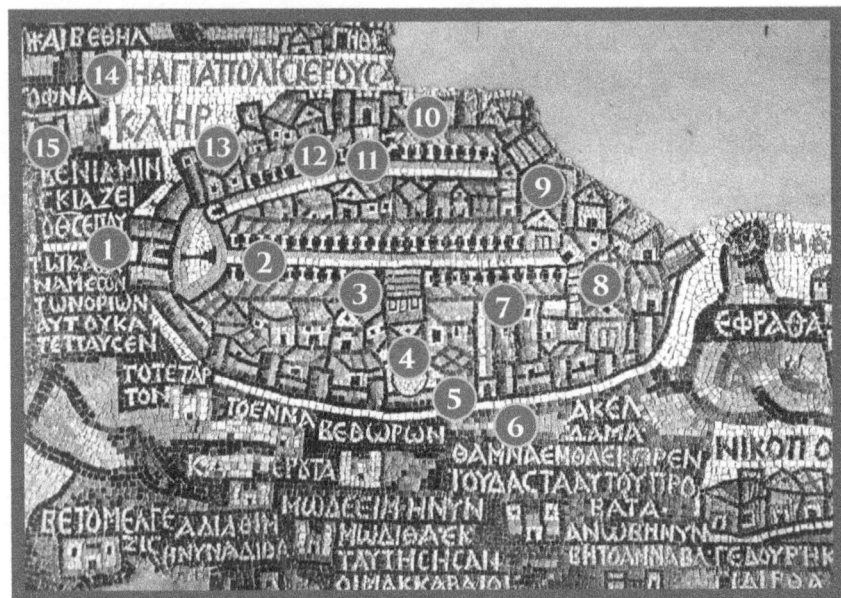

1 - Damascus Gate

2 - Cardo Maxumus 3 - Palace of the Patriarch

4 - Church of Holy Sepulchre

5 - Baptistry of the Church of the Holy Sepulchre

6 - Jaffa Gate

7 - Tower of David

8 - Church of Mount Zion

9 - Nea Church

10 - Temple Area

11 - Lion's Gate / St. Stephen's Gate

12 - Church of the Sheep Pool

13 - Palace of the empress Eudocia

14 - Holy City Jerusalem

15 - Lot of Benjamin

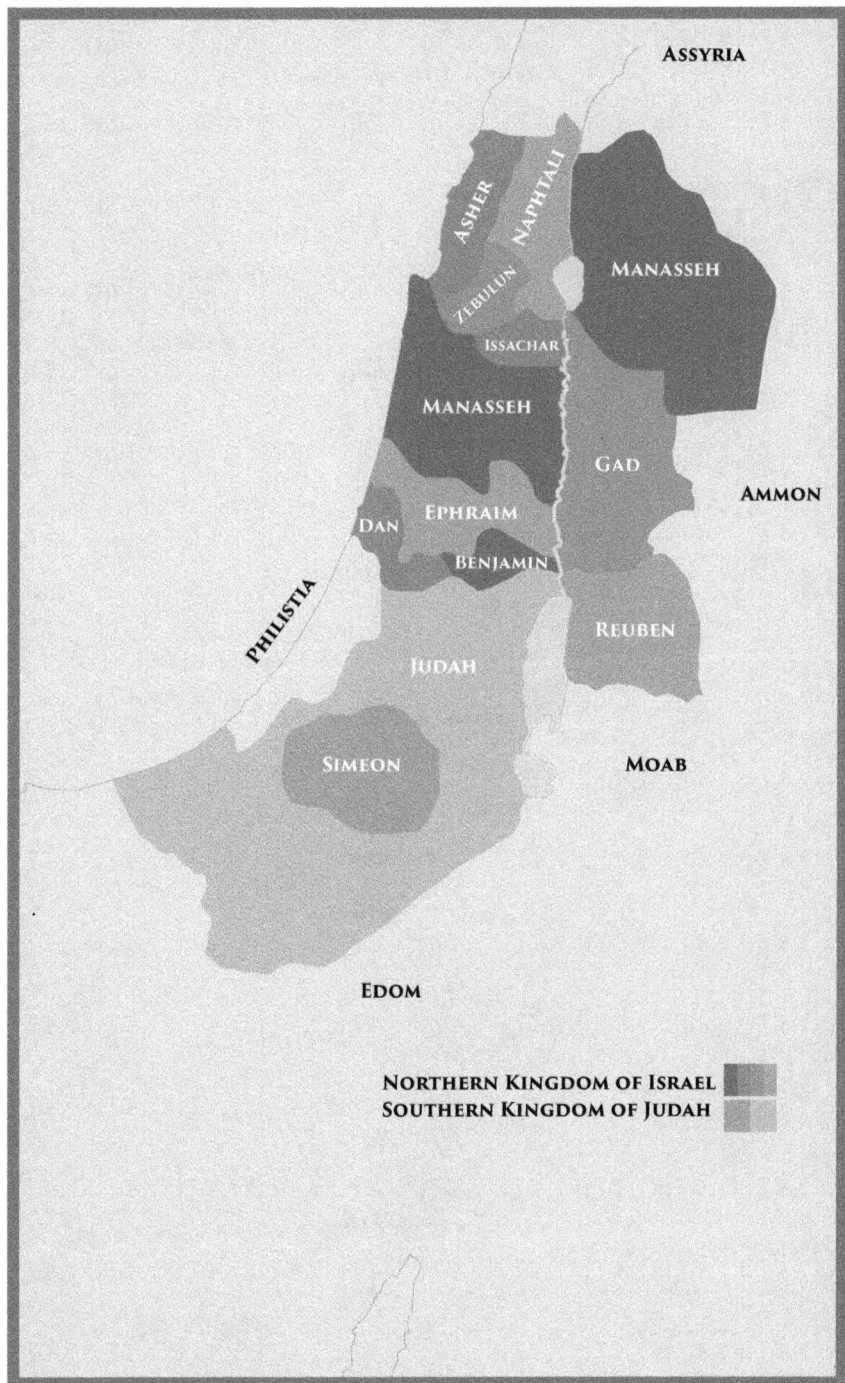

ASSYRIA

ASHER

NAPHTALI

ZEBULUN

MANASSEH

ISSACHAR

MANASSEH

GAD

AMMON

DAN

EPHRAIM

BENJAMIN

PHILISTIA

REUBEN

JUDAH

SIMEON

MOAB

EDOM

NORTHERN KINGDOM OF ISRAEL
SOUTHERN KINGDOM OF JUDAH

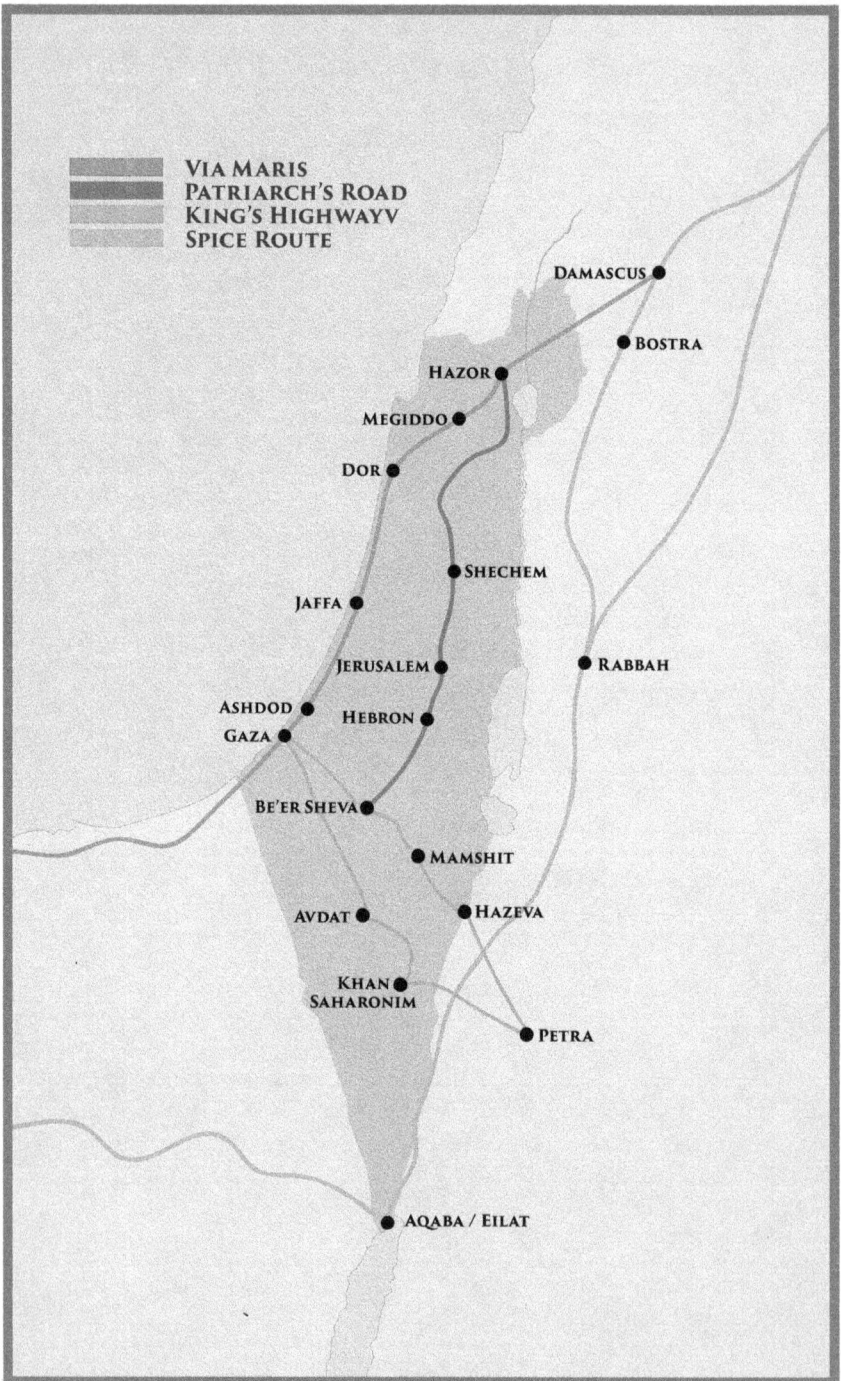

VIA MARIS
PATRIARCH'S ROAD
KING'S HIGHWAYV
SPICE ROUTE

DAMASCUS

BOSTRA

HAZOR

MEGIDDO

DOR

SHECHEM

JAFFA

JERUSALEM

RABBAH

ASHDOD
HEBRON
GAZA

BE'ER SHEVA

MAMSHIT

AVDAT
HAZEVA

KHAN
SAHARONIM

PETRA

AQABA / EILAT

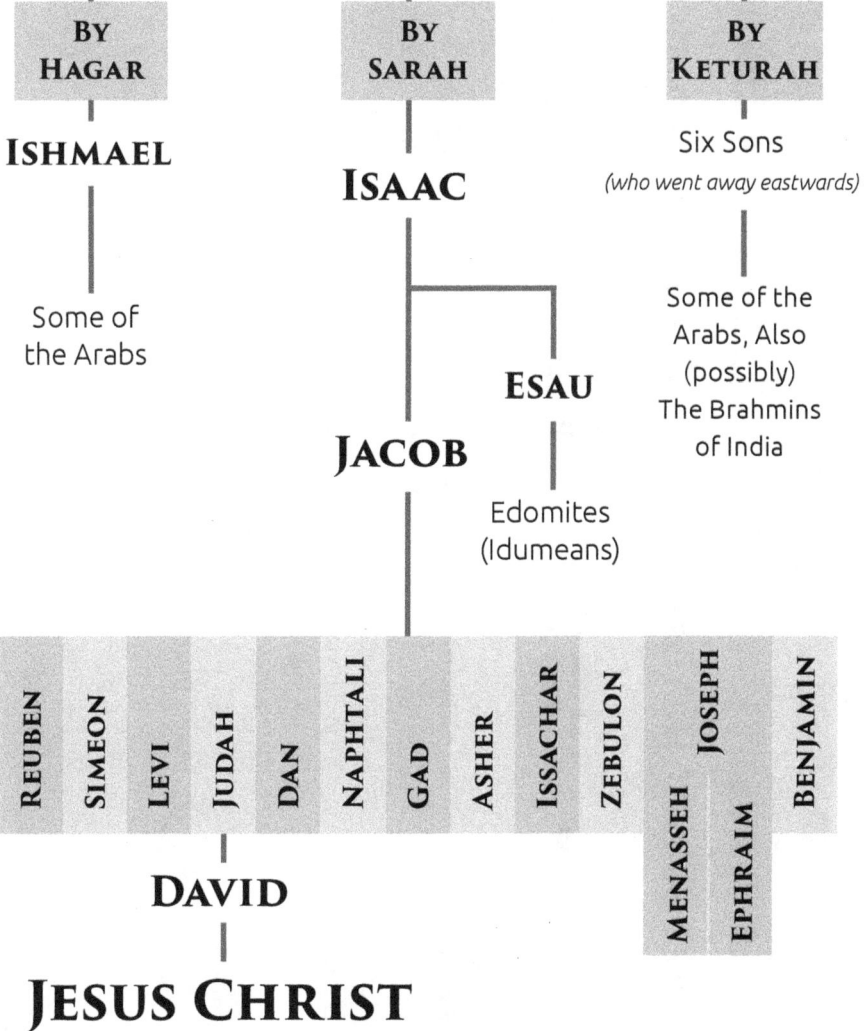

ABRAHAM

*"Look unto the rock from which you were hewn...
Unto Abraham... and Sarah"*

(Isaiah 51:1-2)

BY HAGAR

BY SARAH

BY KETURAH

ISHMAEL

ISAAC

Six Sons
(who went away eastwards)

Some of
the Arabs

ESAU

Some of the
Arabs, Also
(possibly)
The Brahmins
of India

JACOB

Edomites
(Idumeans)

REUBEN | SIMEON | LEVI | JUDAH | DAN | NAPHTALI | GAD | ASHER | ISSACHAR | ZEBULON | MENASSEH | EPHRAIM | JOSEPH | BENJAMIN

DAVID

JESUS CHRIST

THE 39 BOOKS OF THE OT

THE 39 BOOKS OF THE OLD TESTAMENT

17 BOOKS OF HISTORY		5 BOOKS OF WISDOM, POETRY, AND PRAISE	17 BOOKS OF PROPHECY	
5 BOOKS OF LAW	12 BOOKS OF HISTORY		5 BOOKS MAJOR PROPHETS	12 BOOKS MINOR PROPHETS
1. Genesis	6. Joshua	18. Job	23. Isaiah	28. Hosea
2. Exodus	7. Judges	19. Psalms	24. Jeremiah	29. Joel
3. Leviticus	8. Ruth	20. Proverbs	25. Lamentations	30. Amos
4. Numbers	9. 1 Samuel	21. Ecclesiastes	26. Ezekiel	31. Obadiah
5. Deuteronomy	10. 2 Samuel	22. Song of Songs	27. Daniel	32. Jonah
	11. 1 Kings			33. Micah
	12. 2 Kings			34. Nahum
	13. 1 Chronicles			35. Habakkuk
	14. 2 Chronicles			36. Zephaniah
	15. Ezra			37. Haggai
	16. Nehemiah			38. Zechariah
	17. Esther			39. Malachi

9/3 Division based on the Babylonian Exile

OLD TESTAMENT OVERVIEW

ERA		BOOK(S)	HISTORIC EVENTS	THEOLOGY
Prehistory		Gen 1 - 11	• Creation • Fall • Flood • Babel scattering	• Creation blessing • Adam Covenant • Seed Covenant • Shem blessing

Patriarchal	2160 - 1876 BC	Gen 12 - 50	• Call of Abraham
			• Four generations from Abraham
				• Covenant with Abraham:
				  - Heirs
				  - Land
				• Judah blessing

Egyptian Captivity and the Exodus	1876 - 1446 BC	Exod; Lev; Num; Deut	• Moses
			• Plagues
			• Exodus
			• Law
			• Wanderings
				• God remembers and redeems
				• Mosaic Law
				  - Nation of priests
				  - Atonement

Conquest and Judges	1406 - 1050 BC	Josh; Judg; Ruth	• Canaan conquered • Cycle of apostasy	• Fulfillment of land promise • Chaos without a king

United Monarchy	1050 - 931 BC	1, 2 Sam, 1 Kgs 1 - 11;1 Chron - 2 Chron 9;
		Wisdom Literature
			• Saul, David and Solomon
			• Israel's "Golden Age"
				• Covenant with David:
				  - Eternal kingdom
				  - Eternal dynasty

Divided Monarchy	586 - 400 BC	1 Kgs 12 - 2 Kgs, 2 Chron 10 - 36; Hos; Mic; Joel; Amos; Obad; Jon; Nah; Hab; Isa; Zeph; Jer 1 - 26	• Division of Israel from Judah
			• Conquest of Israel (722 BC) and Judah (586 BC)
				• Prophets predict God's temporal judgment and future promise:
				  - Davidic King
				  - Day of the Lord
				  - Servant of the Lord

Exile and Return	586 - 400 BC	Dan; Ezek; Lam; Ezra; Neh; Est; Mal; Zech; Hag; Jer 27 - 52	• Judah in Babylon for 70 years • God restores a remnant in Judah; rebuilds Jerusalem	• New Covenant • Revelation of the future of human history - Triumph of God's kingdom

The Tabernacle

Altar of Incense: The altar of incense symbolizes the "sweet smell" of worship and prayer going up to meet God. It is located in the holy place or priests' room inside the Tabernacle, right outside the Holy of Holies (*Rev 5:8*).

Altar of Sacrifice: A large bronze altar used for bringing atoning sacrifices to God, it stood in the outer courts of the Tabernacle (*Exod 27:1-8*).

Ark of the Covenant: The most sacred of all the items in the Tabernacle, it was located in the Holy of Holies (*1 Sam 5:1-4; 6:1-21; 2 Sam 6*). This chest contained the tablets of the Ten Commandments, as well as Aaron's rod that budded, and a jar of manna (*Heb 9:4*).

Bronze Sea / Bronze Laver: Located at the entrance of the Tabernacle, this basin, made from bronze mirrors was used for ceremonial purifications before entering the sanctuary to serve. It symbolized God's forgiveness after sacrifices were made (*Heb 1:3; John 7:37-39*).

Menorah: A seven-branched golden lampstand which was located in the Holy Place of the Tabenacle. It was to be continuously lighted and symbolizes Jesus, who is the light of the world (*John 1:8-9; 8:12*).

Mercy Seat: The lid of gold on top of the Ark of the Covenant on which the golden cherubim stood. It symbolized God's throne (*Exod 40:20*).

Table of Showbread: Twelve loaves representing the twelve tribes were placed on this golden table in the Holy Place, across from the Lampstand. The Bread of the Presence was placed weekly, and at the end of the week, the priests were to eat it (*1 Sam 21; Mark 2:23-28; John 6:51*).

Veil: the veil that separated the Holy of Holies from the rest of the Tabernacle. Only the High Priest was allowed to enter beyond the veil, but only once a year on Yom Kippur. This veil of the Temple was ripped from top to bottom when Jesus died on the cross, allowing us to come boldly before the throne of God (*Matt 27:50-51; Heb 9:1-9*).

Gold represents the Divine.

Bronze/Copper represents Sin.

THE HOLY OF HOLIES

Mercy Seat

Ark of the Covenant

Veil

Altar of Incense

Menorah

Table of Showbread

THE HOLY PLACE

Bronze Sea

THE OUTER COURT

Altar of Sacrifice

THE "SILENT" 400 YEARS

THE OLD TESTAMENT ENDS WITH REBUILDING THE TEMPLE UNDER THE PERSIANS

In the year 332 BC, Alexander the Great conquers the world, including this region, and introduces Hellenism. After his death, the kingdom is divided into four. The land of Israel, aka Judea, is on the border between the Egyptian and Syrian states. As the border shifts with the international wars, Judea was first under Ptolemies (Egypt) from 300-200 BC; in the year 200 BC, the Seleucid Dynasty (Syria) takes this land.

Significant changes:
- The Old Testament is first translated to Greek: the Septuagint.
- Judea is introduced to Hellenistic culture, Greek language, and religious syncretism

Significant Changes:
- The rise of different Jewish sects.
- Priesthood becomes for sale.
- The king is now both King and High Priest.
- Forced acceptance of Jewish faith.

In 167 BC, the Seleucid ruler Antiochus IV desecrates the Jewish temple. A priestly Hasmonean family, later known as the Maccabees, retaliates by leading a 5-year revolt against the Greeks. Eventually, the Hasmoneans miraculously defeat the Greeks and the event is celebrated annually with Hanukkah.

A dispute between leaders leads to involving the Romans. Plot Twist! Pompey comes with an army and takes control of this region instead, and the Roman Period starts in 63 BC. To prevent another uprising, Romans allow Jewish kings to govern as client-kings. Herod the Great, whose father was an Idumean covert, becomes a client king in Judea in 37 BC.

Significant Changes:
- Herod the Great beautifies and enlarges the Temple and the Temple Mount.
- The brilliant but paranoid king builds fantastic fortresses like Herodion and Masada

THE MESSIAH IS BORN AROUND 4-6 BC

ISRAEL TIMELINE

1948 AD	STATE OF ISRAEL	
1917 AD	BRITISH MANDATE	
1517 AD	OTTOMAN PERIOD	
1260 AD	MAMELUKE PERIOD	
1099 AD	CRUSADERS	
638 AD	MUSLIM PERIOD	
324 AD	BYZANTINE PERIOD	
0	JESUS	
63 BC	ROMAN PERIOD	
167 BC	HASMONEAN PERIOD	
332 BC	HELLENISTIC PERIOD	
538 BC	PERSIAN PERIOD	
586 BC	SHORT BABYLONIAN RULE	
1004 BC	ISRAELITE PERIOD	
1200 BC	JUDGES PERIOD	
3600 BC	CANAANITE PERIOD	

LIFE OF JESUS

Event	Location	Matt.	Mark	Luke	John
Birth of Jesus	Bethlehem	1:18-25		2:1-20	
Childhood	Egypt, Nazareth, and Jerusalem	2:1-23		2:21-52	
Baptism	Jordan River	3:13-17	1:9-11	3:21-22	1:29-34
Temptation	Judean Desert	4:1-11	1:12-13	4:1-13	
First Disciples	Betharba				1:35-51
Water into Wine	Cana				2:1-11
Nicodemus	Jerusalem				3:1-21
Samaritan woman	Sychar in Samaria				4:4-42
Preaching in Synagogues	Galilee	4:17	1:14-15	4:14-15	4:43-45
Moving to Capernaum	Nazareth, Capernaum	4:13-16		4:16-31	
Peter, Andrew, James, and John	Sea of Galilee	4:18-22	1:16-20	5:1-11	
Miracles and Teachings	Galilee	4:23-25	1:35-39	4:42-44	
Heals Simon's Mother-in-Law	Capernaum	8:14-17	1:29-34	4:38-41	
Heals a man with Leprosy	Sea of Galilee, Capernaum	8:1-4	1:40-45	5:12-14	
Heals a Paralysed Man	Capernaum	9:1-8	2:1-12	5:17-26	
Healing at the Pool of Bethesda	Jerusalem				5:1-47
Jesus Appoints the Twelve	Galilee	10:2-4	3:13-19	6:12-19	
Sermon on the Mount	Galilee	5-7		6:12-19	
Heals servant of Centurion	Capernaum	8:5-13		7:1-10	
Raising Widow's Son	Nain			7:11-17	
Anointed by a Forgiven Woman	Capernaum			7:36-50	
Calms the Storm	Sea of Galilee	8:23-27	4:35-41	8:22-25	

EVENT	LOCATION	MATT.	MARK	LUKE	JOHN
Casts out Demons	Gerasenes region	8:28-34	5:1-21	8:26-40	
Raises Jarius' Daughter and Heals the Woman who Touched His Cloak	Galilee (Cana and Capernaum)	9:20-22	5:25-34	8:43-48	
Feeding the 5,000	Bethsaida	14:13-21	6:32-44	9:10-17	6:1-13
Walks on Water	Sea of Galilee	14:22-33	6:45-51		6:16-21
Peter's Confession of Christ	Caesarea-Philippi	16:13-20	8:27-30	9:18-22	
Transfiguration	Mt. Hermon	17:1-8	9:2-8	9:28-36	
Forgives Woman Caught in Adultery	Jerusalem				8:2-11
Visits with Mary and Martha	Bethany on Mt. of Olives			10:38-42	
Heals a Man Born Blind	Pool of Siloam, Jerusalem				9:1-7
Raises Lazarus from the Dead	Bethany on Mt. of Olives				11:1-44
Heals Ten People with Leprosy	Jerusalem			17:11-19	
Speaks with the Rich Young Man	Jerusalem	19:16-30	10:17-31	18:18-30	
Zaccheus the Tax Collector	Jericho			19:1-10	
Palm Sunday	Jerusalem	21:1-11	11:1-10	19:28-38	12:12-15
Clears the Temple	Temple Mount	21:12-13	11:15-17	19:45-46	
The Last Supper	Upper Room in Jerusalem	26:17-30	14:12-26	22:7-38	13:1-30
In the Garden of Gethsemane	Gethsemane on Mt of Olives	26:36-56	14:32-50	22:39-53	18:1-11
Crucifixion	Jerusalem	27:26-66	15:15-47	23:24-56	19:16-42
Resurrection and Ascension	Jerusalem & Mt. of Olives	28	16	24	20

DAY	EVENT	SCRIPTURE
Sunday	Palm Sunday - Jesus' Royal Welcome into Jerusalem	Matt 21:1-9 Mark 11:1-10 Luke 19:28-44 John 12:12-50
Monday	Jesus Curses the Fig Tree & Clears the Temple Courts	Matt 21:12-19 Mark 11:12-17 Luke 19:45-46
Tuesday	Withered Fig Tree. Temple Controversy. Widow's Offering. Olivet Discourse.	Matt 21:20-27, 46 Mark 11:20-13:37 Luke 20:1-21, 36
Wednesday	Jesus is Anointed at Bethany	Matt 26:6-15 Mark 14:1-11 Luke 22:1-6 John 12:2-11
Thursday	Last Supper. Gethsemane. Jesus is Betrayed, Arrested, and Tried Before the Sanhedrin. Peter's Denial	Matt 26:17-75 Mark 14:12-72 Luke 22:7-65; John 18:1-27
Friday	Jesus is Convicted, Crucified and Buried	Matt 27:1-61 Mark 15:1-47 Luke 22:66-23:56 John 18:28-19:37
Saturday	The Tomb is Sealed	Matt 27:62-66
Sunday	Jesus is Alive!	Matt 28:1-15 Mark 16:1-8 Luke 24:1-49 John 20:1-23

CITY WALL IN THE TIME OF JESUS

OLD CITY WALL TODAY

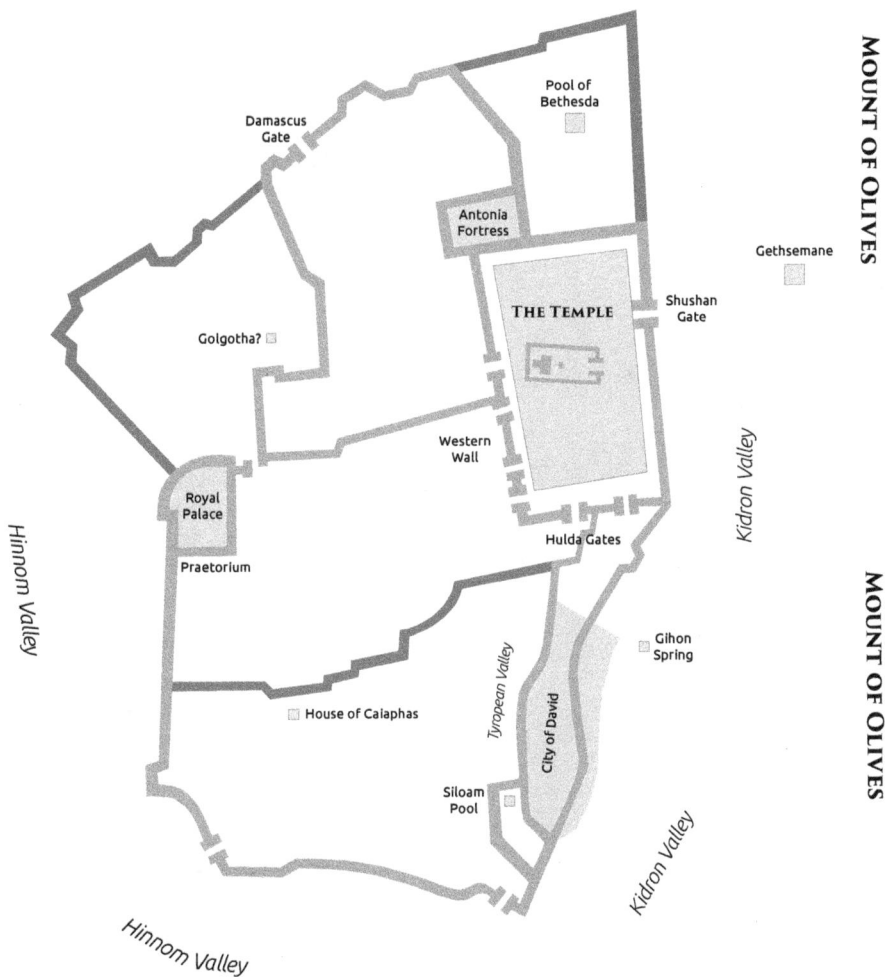

MOUNT OF OLIVES

Pool of
Bethesda

Damascus
Gate

Antonia
Fortress

Gethsemane

THE TEMPLE

Shushan
Gate

Golgotha?

Western
Wall

Kidron Valley

Royal
Palace

Praetorium

Hulda Gates

Hinnom Valley

MOUNT OF OLIVES

Gihon
Spring

Tyropean Valley

City of David

House of Caiaphas

Siloam
Pool

Kidron Valley

Hinnom Valley

200 yards

200 m

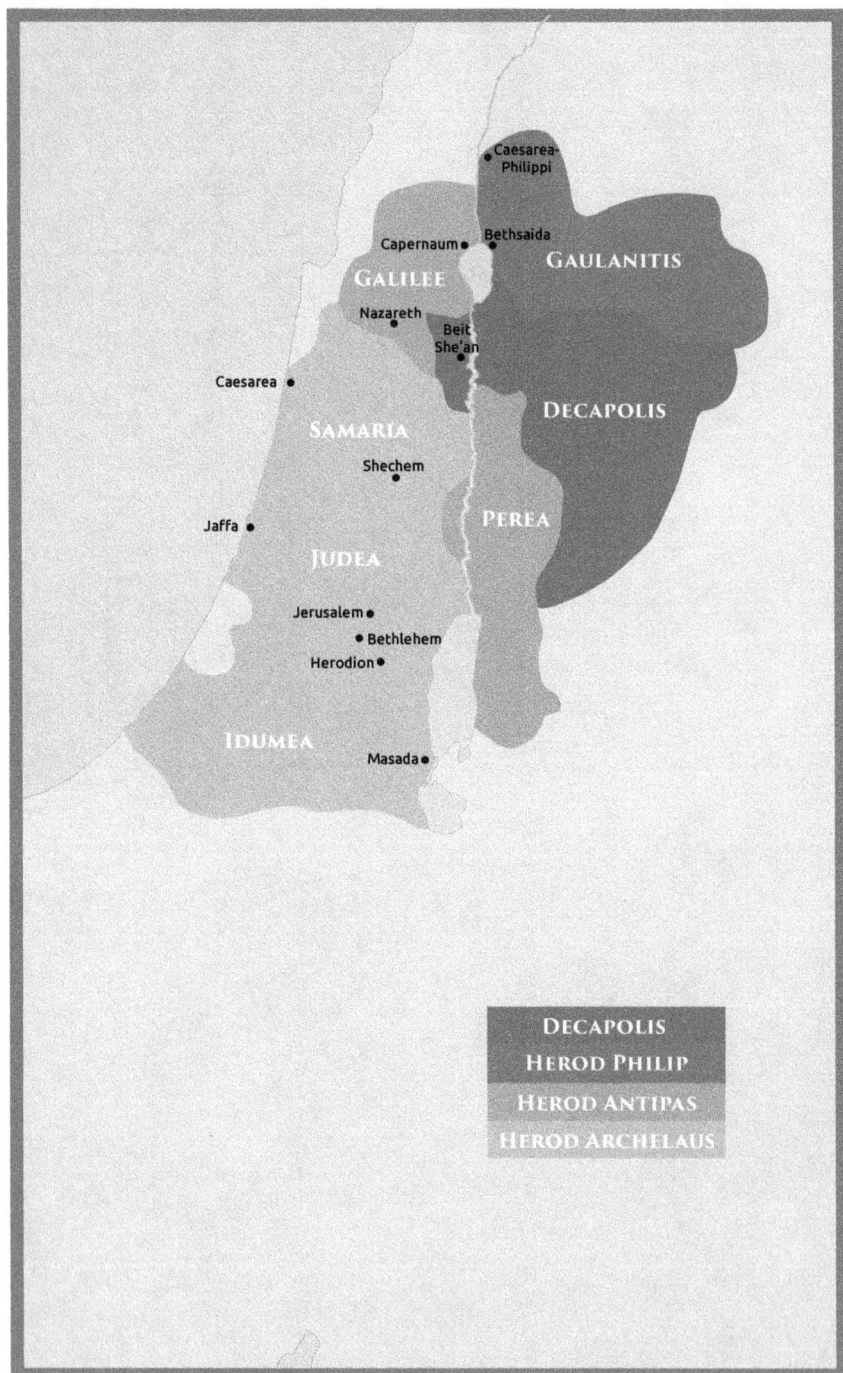

Caesarea-
Philippi

Capernaum • Bethsaida

GALILEE

GAULANITIS

Nazareth
Beit
She'an

Caesarea •

DECAPOLIS

SAMARIA

Shechem

PEREA

Jaffa •

JUDEA

Jerusalem •
• Bethlehem
Herodion •

IDUMEA

Masada •

DECAPOLIS
HEROD PHILIP
HEROD ANTIPAS
HEROD ARCHELAUS

JEWISH SECTS OF THE 1ST CENTURY

	PHARISEES	SADDUCEES	ESSENES	ZEALOTS
IDENTITY	• Prushim - "set aside" Paresh - "to interpret" • Middle class citizens consisting of rabbis and sages. They later become mainstream Orthodox Jews and write the Mishnah and Talmud.	• Tzdokim - "righteous". Descendants of Zadok the first high priest of the temple. • Exclusively an aristocratic group, the Sadducees were involved in political matters.	• Eseim - unknown origin. • People from every society who chose to live a life set apart. • The Dead Sea Scrolls were believed to have been written by a group of Essenes.	• Kana'im - Zelotes (greek) "one who is zealous on behalf of God." • Extreme Pharisees and religious Jews, primarily from the Galilee.
BELIEFS	• Freewill • Resurrection and life after death • Hellenism is a necessary evil • Prophecy/Revelation finished • Entire Old Testament (TaNaKh) and Oral Law	• Freewill • No resurrection or life after death • Accept Hellenism • Prophecy/Revelation finished • The Torah only, against Oral Law	• Predestination • No resurrection but there is life after death • Against Hellenism • Prophecy and Revelation still continues in the present • Entire Old Testament, against Oral Law • Against priestly corruption of Temple practices	• Theology closely followed that of the Pharisees. • Violently against Rome • God is the only ruler • Slavery is worse than death
PRACTICES	• Particularly involved in synagogues in Torah Study • Interpretation of law to apply to advancing daily life • Part of the Sanhedrin council	• As priests ran the Temple and all the ceremonies • Lived Hellenistic lifestyles with Roman support • Dominated the Sanhedrin council	• Lived in isolated communities with shared property and the sacred communal meals • Practiced Ritual purification • Worked on copying and studying the Torah	• Practiced terrorism against the Romans. • The extreme of the extremes were called Sicarii (sicae - "dagger") - they also opposed anyone who viewed beliefs differently.

FEAST / HOLIDAY	DATE OBSERVED	EVENT STORY & HOW IT IS CELEBRATED
PASSOVER פֶּסַח Pesach (PAY-sahk)	Nisan 14th (March or April)	Commemorates God's Deliverance of Israel out of Egypt. A perfect lamb was slain, and its blood was painted on the doorposts so that the punishment of the angel of the LORD will "pass over" the homes of the children of Israel. (*Lev 23:4,5; Exod 12:15-20; Deut 16:16; Matt 26:17-30*).
UNLEAVENED BREAD חַג הַמַּצּוֹת Hag HaMatzot	Nisan 15th-21st (March or April)	Considered as part of the Passover celebration (along with Firstfruits) The LORD commanded that for 7 days, the Israelites are not to eat bread with yeast, to remember their ancestors who left Egypt in haste. Before the celebrations start, the people of Israel have to clean their house of any yeast which symbolizes sin. Instead of bread, they eat Matzah. (*Lev 23:6-8; Exod 12:15-20; Isa 53:2*).
FIRSTFRUITS יוֹם הַבִּכּוּרִים Yom HaBikkurim	Visan 16th (March or April)	Taking place during the Passover celebrations, the people offer the first ripe sheaf of barley as an offering to dedicate the harvest to the LORD. This happens on the third day of Passover, the same day of the Resurrection. (*Lev 23:19-14; 1 Cor 15:20,22,23*).
WEEKS / PENTECOST שָׁבֻעוֹת Shavuot	Sivan 6th (May or June)	Fifty days after Passover, also known as Pentecost, a new offering to the LORD is presented, a grain offering of the summer wheat harvest. Pentecost is also believed to have been the same time that God gave Moses the 10 commandments. It is a Feast of joy and thankfulness for the LORD's blessing. (*Lev 23:15-22; Deut 16:16; Acts 2*).
TRUMPETS / NEW YEAR רֹאשׁ הַשָּׁנָה Rosh Hashana	Tishrei 1st (September or October)	Trumpets are blown to remind people to repent of their sins as the Day of Atonement is approaching. Jewish tradition says that according to their good deeds, they will be inscribed in the Book of Life for another year on Yom Kippur. Rosh Hashana is a serious holiday, yet Israel celebrates it with apples and honey for a "prosperous and sweet" new year. (*Lev 23:23-25; Rev 20:15*).

DAY OF ATONEMENT כִּפּוּר יוֹם Yom Kippur	Tishrei 10th (September or October)	In Biblical times, this was the only day the High Priest entered the Holy of Holies to atone for the people's sins. A scapegoat is then released into the wilderness to signify that their sins were carried away. In Israel today, Yom Kippur is a national fasting day, everything is closed, including transportation. (*Lev 23:26-32; Luke 23:44-46*).
BOOTHS / TABERNACLES סֻכּוֹת Sukkot	Tishrei 15th-21st (September or October)	The Feast of Tabernacles commemorates Israel's 40 years in the desert. It is a week-long celebration where the people of Israel build and live in temporary booths, sukkot, to remember God's Faithfulness and protection. A water ceremony is included as part of the prayer for rain. (*Lev 23:33-43; Deut 16:16: John 7:13-14*).
REJOICING IN THE LAW הַתּוֹרָה שִׂמְחַת Simchat Torah	Tishrei 22nd or 23rd (September or October)	The eighth and final day of Sukkot is appointed by God as a sacred assembly. Today, it is celebrated as the completion of reading the Torah (the Law) for that year and the cycle starts again with Genesis for the next year. (*Lev 23:36; John 1:1,14*).
DEDICATION חֲנֻכָּה Hanukkah	Kislev 25th – Tevet 2nd (November or December)	The Feast of Hanukkah celebrates the victory of the Maccabees over the Greeks in 165 BC. It is also known as the Feast of Lights because of the legendary provision of oil for the temple. The oil was supposed to last one day, but the flame miraculously burned for eight days. A Chanukiah (a 9-branched menorah) is lit during these eight days. (*John 10:22-23, also in Maccabees*).
FEAST OF LOTS פוּרִים Purim	Adar 14th or 15th (February or March)	Purim, also known as Feast of Lots, celebrates God's deliverance of the Jews in the Persian kingdom from Haman's wicked plot. It is celebrated by the interactive reading of the scroll of Esther, spending time with family and friends, giving gifts to the poor, and costume festivities. (*Book of Esther*).

"Three times a year all your men must appear before the Lord your God [in Jerusalem]: at the Festival of Unleavened Bread, the Festival of Weeks, and the Festival of Tabernacles." (Deut 16:16).

147

THE SEVEN SPECIES

Wheat, barley, grapes, figs, pomegranates, olives, dates
"For the Lord your God is bringing you into a good land—a land with brooks, streams, and deep springs gushing out into the valleys and hills; a land with wheat and barley, vines and fig trees, pomegranates, olive oil and honey." *(Deut 8:7-8).*

ACACIA TREE

(Exod 25-27; 30:1-5; 35:7,24; 36:20,31,36; 37; 38:1,6; Deut 10:3; Isa. 41:19)
Acacia trees are known to thrive in the wilderness under hot and dry climates. Their wood, being hard and durable, was used in the building of the tabernacle and the different sacred items inside.

ALMOND TREE

(Gen 43:11; Exod 25:33-34; 37:19-20; Num 17; Eccl 12:5; Jer 1:11)
The Almond Tree is of the first to blossom after winter with striking white, pink, or purple flowers. The LORD chose Aaron, from the house of Levi, as high priest by sprouting his staff with buds, blossoms, and almonds.

BARLEY

(Deut 8:8; Judg 7:13; Ruth 1:22; 2:17,23; 3:2,15,17; 2 Sam 14:30; 2 Sam 21:9; 2 Kgs 7:1,16,18; 1 Chr 11:13; Ezek 4:9; John 6:9,13)
Barley ripens faster than wheat and can grow in less fertile soil, making it cheaper than wheat. When Jesus fed the 5,000, it is mentioned that they were five loaves of barley bread, which was the main food of the poor people at the time. Barley is usually ready for harvest around April.

BROOM TREE

(Gen 21; 1 Kgs 19:4-5; Job 30:4; Ps 120:4)
The Broom tree, also known as Rotem, is a large desert bush that is known for providing good shade and therefore a place of refuge from the desert sun. Its wood, which has long-burning qualities, makes it a great source for charcoal.

CAROB TREE

(Mark 1:6 (?); Luke 15:16 (?))
Carob trees are very common in the land of the Bible and are most known for their 6 inch long pods which can be used to make sweet syrup. Scholars believe the syrup is the 'wild honey' that John the Baptist ate while in the wilderness.

FIG TREE
(Gen 3:7; Judg 9:10-11; 1 Sam 30:11-12; 1 Kgs 4:25; Ps 105:33; Prov 27:18; Isa 34:4; 36:16; Jer 24:1-10; Hos 9:10; Nah 3:12; Zech 3:10; Matt 21:19-21; Mark 120-21; 13:28; Luke 13:6-7; 21:29-31; John 1:47-51; Jas 3:12; Rev 6:13)
The Fig Tree is mentioned over 50 times in the Scriptures and usually in the context of symbolizing of prosperity and well being.

GRAPE VINE
(Gen 40:9-12; Lev 19:10; Num 6:1-4; 13:23-27; 15:5; Deut 6:11; 23:24; Judg 6:11; Ps 4:7; Eccl 9:7; Isa 63:3; 65:8; Jer 48:33; Amos 9:13; Matt 7:15-16; 26:27-28; Mark 2:22; John 2:1-11; 15:1-5; 19:28-29; Jas 3:12)
Even before the Israelites came into Canaan, the land was abundant in vineyards. When the spies first scouted the land, they brought back clusters of grapes so large that they needed to be carried on a stick between two people. Additionally, the vine and branches commonly refer to the believers being grafted into the grapevine symbolizing Jesus. The night before Jesus died, he instructed his followers to remember him by eating bread and drinking wine together.

HYSSOP PLANT
(Exod 12:22; Lev 14:4,6,49-52; Num 19:6,18; 1 Kgs 4:33; Ps 51:7; John 19:29; Heb 9:19)
The Hyssop plant was commonly used in scripture as a brush or an instrument for carrying a sponge. This is the same plant that the Hebrews used to paint blood on the doorposts at the Exod. The wine-vinegar-soaked sponge was lifted to Jesus on a Hyssop plant.

OAK TREE (ALON)
(Gen 13:18; 18:1; 35:8; Josh 19:33; Isa 6:13; 61::1-3; Hos 4:12-13)
The mighty oak tree stands out from its surroundings and is commonly mentioned as a reference point such as Abraham and Sarah pitching their tents by the "great oaks of Mamre." It is no wonder that this mighty tree is also used as a symbol of righteousness.

OLIVE TREE
(Gen 8:11; Exod 30:23-25; Deut 6:11; 8:8; 24:20; 28:40; Judg 9:8-9; 2 Kgs 18:32; Ps 52:8; 128:3; Jer 11:16; Hos 14:6; Amos 4:9; Zech 4:3,11-14; Matt 26:36; Luke 22:39; Rom 11:17,24; Rev 11:4)
This evergreen tree gets its name from the abundant oil that it produces. Oil is very important in the Bible as it represents the spirit of God and used in the anointing of kings and priests. The Olive Tree is one of the most valuable trees in antiquity, and its branch became a symbol of peace ever since the time of Noah. Olive wood is very hard and beautiful, allowing for the manufacture of different wooden objects from furniture to souvenir wooden sculptures.

PALM TREE

(Deut 34:3; Lev 23:40-42; Judg 4:5; Ps 92:12, Song 7:7; Ezek 41:18; Matt 21:8; John 12:13)

With its tall upright structure and flourishing branches, the Palm Tree has long been a symbol of victory. At Jesus' triumphal entry to Jerusalem, the people welcomed him waving palm branches and crying "Hosanna!".

POMEGRANATE

(Exod 28:33-34; 39:24; Num 13:23-27; 20:5; 1 Sam 14:2; 1 Kgs 7:18,20,42; Song 4:13; 6:7; 7:12; 8:2; Jer 52:22-23; Joel 1:11-12)

The pomegranate is a very peculiar fruit made up of leathery outer skin, full of jewel-like seeds inside, and has a crown on top. This blood-red beauty was used in many designs in the tabernacle, temple, and on priests clothing.

TAMARISK TREE

(Gen 21:33; 1 Sam 22:6; 31:13)

Abraham is mentioned to have specifically planted a Tamarisk tree in Beer Sheva, and there he called on the name of the Lord, the Eternal God.

TEREBINTH (ELAH) TREE

(Gen 35:4; Josh 24:26; Judg 6:11,19; 1 Sam 17; 2 Sam 18:9-10,14; 1 Kgs 13:14; 1 Chr 10:12; Isa 1:30; 6:13; Ezek 6:13; Hos 4:12-13)

The Terebinth, also known as Elah or Pistachio, is a monumental tree usually associated with a sacred site or a burial place. The Elah Valley, where the story of David and Goliath took place, may have been named after this tree.

WHEAT

(Gen 41:5; Exod 9:31-32; 34:22; 29:2-3; Lev 23:14; Judg 6:11; Ruth 2:23; 1 Sam 6:13; 1 Chr 21:18-28; Ps 147:12-14; Mic 4:12; Matt 3:11-12; 13:8,24-30; Mark 2:23; Luke 22:31-32; John 12:24)

Wheat in the Bible has much spiritual significance. Aside from its practical use in making bread, which symbolizes life, the threshing of wheat is often used as a symbol of God's coming judgment on sin. The Festival of Weeks, also known as Shavuot, celebrates offering the firstfruits of the wheat harvest and is one of the three pilgrimage feasts required to be celebrated in Jerusalem.

CAMEL
(Gen 24:10; Lev 11:4; Isa 30:6; Matt 3:4; 19:24; 23:24)
"The ship of the desert." Because of their incredible ability of endurance and persistence, the camel was used as a mode of transportation throughout history and often associated with wealth and riches. The camels of southern Israel usually belong to Bedouins.

DONKEY
(Exod 13:13; Num 22:21-41; Judg 15:15-17; Ps 104:10-12; Isa 1:3; Zech 9:9; Matt 21:1-3)
A symbol of the people, often a part of everyday life of agriculture and trade, Jesus humbly chose to ride a donkey into Jerusalem. Gifted with cautiousness, many of the ancient paths in and around the villages were made by donkeys as they traversed the hillsides.

DOVE
(Gen 8:8; 2 Kgs 6:25; Song 2:14; Isa 38:14; Jer 48:28; Matt 3:16; 10:16; John 2:16)
The dove has been a symbol of the divine since antiquity, the Word of God even says "the Holy Spirit descended upon Jesus like a dove." Many columbariums, or dovecotes, have been discovered in excavations throughout Israel and they indicate the Biblical traditions of the number of doves sacrificed at the Temple as atonement for sin.

EAGLE/VULTURE
(Exod 19:4; Lam 4:19; Isa 40:31; Jer 48:40; Ezek 1:10; Dan 7:4; Revelation 4:7; 12:14)
When the Bible mentions the eagle, it is most likely referring to the large Griffon Vultures found in the land. The eagle represents strength, freedom, and power and is usually mentioned in the context of promises from God to his beloved people.

GAZELLE
(Deut 12:15; 14:5; 1 Chr 12:8; Prov 6:5; Song 2:9,17; 4:5; 8:14)
Gazelles, which are smaller than deer, are known for their beauty and swift agility by which they can escape from hunters. These shy creatures can be spotted nearly anywhere in Israel but mostly found in the Dead Sea Region.

HYRAX
(Ps 104:18)
Hyraxes, also known as rock badgers, can be seen primarily in the region of Ein Gedi. They live in groups of about 10-80 and find their refuge in the rocks and crags.

IBEX
(1 Sam 24:1-2; Ps 104:18)
With breathtaking agility, Ibexes (also known as the Biblical wild goat) can be seen scaling almost vertical cliffs in the Ein Gedi region. They are mentioned in the Scriptures as those to whom the high mountains belong.

OWL
(Lev 11:17; Ps 102:6; Isa 34:10-15)
These nocturnal creatures are commonly found among the ruins at different sites throughout Israel. Their hooting cries resemble the sounds of mourning over the destruction of the cities.

RAVEN
(Gen 8:7; Lev 11:15; 1 Kgs 17:4-6; Ps 147:7-9; Song 5:11; Luke 12:24)
With a high sense of orientation, the raven was one of the birds that Noah let out of the ark to search for land. Although in other cultures the raven is referred to in a negative light, the Bible compares God's provision for His people with the way He feeds the ravens. He even directed the ravens to bring food to Elijah while he was hiding in Kerith Ravine.

SPARROW
(Ps 84:3; 102:7; Matt 6:25-34; 10:29-31; Luke 12:24)
Though abundant and very common in the land of Israel, Jesus tells us that each one of these sparrows is important to God, how much more valuable are we!

GATES OF JERUSALEM

Damascus - one of the main gates on the north side of the city, and the most impressive. As its name suggests, the road in front of it led to Damascus, the great city from which many of Jerusalem's rulers once came.

Jaffa - the main western gate leading to and from Jaffa or Joppa. Pilgrims disembarking from Jaffa port would have come straight through this gate, which is why it still leads to the most popular parts of the market.

Golden (Beautiful) - the main eastern gate that led to the Temple Mount. Blocked in today, it is traditionally the location of the gate from which Jesus entered Jerusalem on Palm Sunday. (*Matt 21:1-11*) It is also known as the Gate of Mercy.

St Stephen's (Lions) - this eastern gate is the traditional location of the stoning of Stephen (*Acts 7:54-60*). It is near the Sheep Gate of the New Testament, which is another possibility for the triumphal entry (*Matt 21:1-11*).

Herod (Flowers)- located on the north-eastern corner of the Old City, this modest gate gets its name from the belief that King Herod's palace may have been nearby. In Arabic, the name for Flowers Gate sounds similar to "awakened" which may refer to the nearby cemetery and the hope of the resurrection.

Zion - bearing Jerusalem's earliest biblical name, it is located on the south side of the wall, adjacent to Mt Zion. It is also known as the Gate of the Prophet David, as the Tomb of King David is a few steps away.

Dung - situated at the lowest point of the walls and close to the Temple Mount, (*Neh 3:13*), it may indeed have been used to remove refuse and possibly ashes from the Temple.

New - the only Old City entryway not part of its original design, New Gate was added in the 16th century to allow Christians easier access to the Holy Sites.

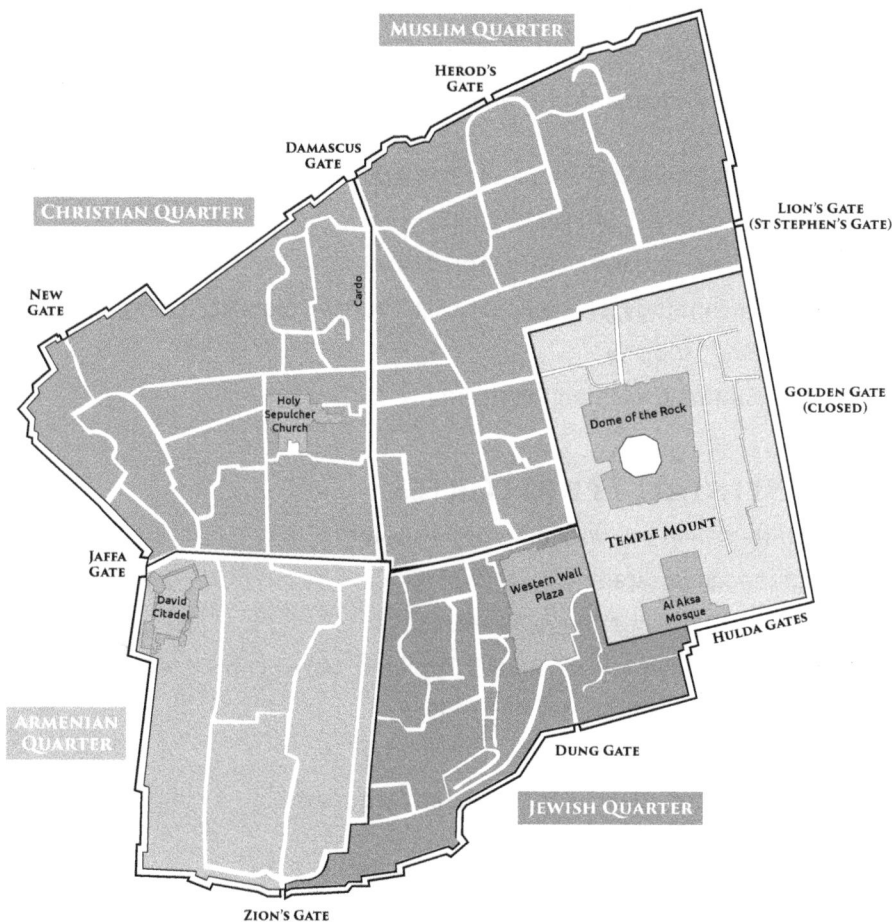

MUSLIM QUARTER

HEROD'S
GATE

DAMASCUS
GATE

CHRISTIAN QUARTER

LION'S GATE
(ST STEPHEN'S GATE)

NEW
GATE

Cardo

GOLDEN GATE
(CLOSED)

Holy
Sepulcher
Church

Dome of the Rock

TEMPLE MOUNT

JAFFA
GATE

David
Citadel

Western Wall
Plaza

Al Aksa
Mosque

HULDA GATES

ARMENIAN
QUARTER

DUNG GATE

JEWISH QUARTER

ZION'S GATE

155

ISRAEL

Capital: Jerusalem

Official Languages: Hebrew and Arabic

Government: Parliamentary Democracy (120 in Knesset like Great Assembly)

Population: 9.1 million (75% Jews, 21% Arab, 4% other)

Currency: New Israeli Shekel (ILS/NIS)

Major Religions: Judaism, Islam, Christianity

Industry: Technology, pharmaceuticals, tourism, manufacturing, military

National Bird: Hoopoe

National Flower: Cyclamen Persicum

PALESTINIAN TERRITORIES

Capital: Ramallah but with aim for Jerusalem

Official Language: Arabic

Government: Parliamentary Democracy

Population: 4 million (West Bank 2.2 million, Gaza Strip 1.8 million)

Currency: New Israeli Shekel (ILS / NIS)

Major Religions: Islam, Christianity

Industry: Tourism, quarrying, small family business

GENERAL INFO

Time Difference: 8 hours ahead of Central Time

Currency conversion:

1 US Dollar = 3.5 ILS
1 British Pound = 4.4 ILS
1 Euro = 3.9 ILS

Temperate Climate:

	Jerusalem	Tel Aviv	Haifa	Safed	Tiberius	Dead Sea
January	43-54° F	48-66° F	46-63° F	37-50° F	48-65° F	53-69° F
	6-12° C	9-19° C	8-17° C	3-10° C	9-18° C	12-21° C
March	47-61° F	51-68° F	47-70° F	43-55° F	51-72° F	60-78° F
	8-16° C	11-20° C	8-21° C	6-13° C	11-22° C	16-26° C
July	67-83° F	70-87° F	68-86° F	65-84° F	72-98° F	83-102° F
	19-28° C	21-31° C	20-30° C	18-29° C	22-37° C	28-39° C
November	54-66° F	55-75° F	56-73° F	54-66° F	59-78° F	65-80° F
	12-19° C	13-24° C	13-23° C	12-19° C	15-26° C	18-27° C

IDF

IDF - The Israel Defence Force is the army of the State of Israel.

- Started May 1948.

- Mandatory after age 18 but exceptions can be made on religious, physical, or psychological grounds. Arab citizens are also exempt if they so choose. The Ultra-Orthodox are exempt from service by the Tal Law, but this has been disputed in several court cases.

- Men serve 2 years and 8 months, up to 3 years. Women serve 2 years. (Israel is one of only a few nations that conscript and deploy women in combat roles).

- Those who serve receive lots of benefits such as university scholarships, tax reduction and health insurance benefits.

ISRAEL'S DIVERSE POPULATION

SECULAR JEW

They hold on to their identity as a Jewish culture mixed in with modern society, without the faith of their ancestors. Makeup over 40% of the Jewish population.

ULTRA-ORTHODOX JEW

Jews that are pro-religious coercion and emphasize studying the Torah and Talmud. Many of them do not recognize the State of Israel as legitimate and do not join the IDF.

NATIONAL RELIGIOUS JEW

Recognize the modern state as a legitimate entity yet still desire for Israel to become a religious state.

JEWISH BELIEVER IN JESUS

Also known as Messianic Jews, they preserve the Jewish culture yet accept Jesus as their Lord and Savior. Around 20,000.

PALESTINIAN JEW

Jews that lived in the land before the foundation of the State of Israel in 1948 and speak Arabic fluently.

ARAB MUSLIM

18% of the population in Israel.

MUSLIM BACKGROUND BELIEVER (MBB)

Over 300 in Israel. They are usually not publicly announced as they are in danger of their neighbors and families.

ARAB ISRAELIS

Arabs who own an Israeli ID. Most self-designate themselves as Palestinians by nationality and Israeli by citizenship, while others prefer "Israeli Arab".

ARAB CHRISTIAN

Around 175,000 Arab Christians in Israel. They enjoy a variety of denominational backgrounds such as Baptist, Roman Catholic, Greek Orthodox, Anglican, Baptist, Melchite, and others.

ARMENIANS

Part of the Armenian Diaspora, around 800 Armenians live in the Armenian quarter of the Old City and 10,000 in Israel.

DRUZE

An offshoot of Islam who have a secret religion and are loyal to the State of Israel. 104,000 in population, most in northern Israel.

BEDOUIN

Nomadic Arab tribes who mostly live in the desert and have the highest fertility rate in the world. Many of them volunteer in the IDF.

PALESTINIAN MUSLIM

Makeup 99% of the PA areas.

PALESTINIAN CHRISTIAN

Only 1% of the Palestinian population. Leaving the land because of Islamic persecution.

REFUGEES & ASYLUM SEEKERS

From Sudan, the Philippines, China, Kosovo, Thailand, even Christian Lebanese soldiers from the 1981 war.

IMMIGRANT

Jews from all over the world who made Aliyah to Israel, 37% of the population.

ALAWITE

An offshoot of Shia Islam who have their own set of beliefs and in Israel live mainly in the village of Ghajar. They are originally from Syria from the same community of the Al-Assad family who is governing Syria.

EXPATRIATE

Mostly found in Jerusalem.

JERUSALEM SYNDROME SUFFERER

People from either Jewish or Christian backgrounds who see themselves as prophetic biblical figures when visiting Israel.

SAMARITANS

Israel's smallest religious minority and own an Israeli ID. Assimilated descendants of the Assyrians and residents of the district of Samaria who consider themselves the original Jews and recognize their own version of the Pentateuch plus the book of Joshua.

THE HEBREW LETTERS

Name & Sound	Letter	Value	Literal Meaning	Symbolic meaning
Aleph (vowel)	א	1	ox, bull, thousand	strength, leader, first
Bet / Vet B, V	ב	2	tent, house	household, in, into, family
Gimel G	ג	3	camel	to lift up, pride, self-will
Dalet D	ד	4	door	pathway, to enter
Hey H	ה	5	window, behold	'the', to reveal
Vav V	ו	6	nail, peg	'and', to add, to secure, join together
Zayin Z	ז	7	weapon	cut, to cut off, pierce
Chet CH	ח	8	fence, hedge, chamber	private, to separate, protect
Tet T	ט	9	snake	To surround, coil, twist
Yood Y	י	10	closed hand	work, a deed done, to make
Kaf K, CH	כ	20	open hand, wing	to cover, to open, to allow, power
Lamed L	ל	30	cattle goad, staff	authority, control, urge forward, teach
Mem M	מ	40	water	liquid, massive, mighty, chaos
Noon N	נ	50	fish (moving)	activity, live, faithfulness

Samech S	ס	60	prop	support, twist slowly, turn
Ayin '	ע	70	eye, fountain	To see, know, experience, understand
Pey P, F	פ	80	mouth	To speak, word, open, beginning, here
Tsadik TS	צ	90	fishhook	catch, desire, harvest, righteous
Koof Q, K	ק	100	back of the head	behind, last, least, final
Reysh R	ר	200	head	A person, head, highest, first,
Sheen S, SH	ש	300	teeth	consume, destroy
Tav T	ת	400	sign, mark, cross	to seal, covenant, last

*ch is pronounced as in Bach

REVIVAL OF THE HEBREW LANGUAGE

Hebrew is the only ancient language that has ever been successfully revived. Ever since Biblical times and up until the 19th century, Hebrew was only studied as a sacred language.

With the spirit of Zionism on the rise in Europe and many Jewish people returning to the land of Israel, Eliezer Ben-Yehuda decides there is a need to unify the people with a common language. In 1881, Ben-Yehuda starts speaking exclusively in Hebrew with family and friends. Quickly realizing that the ancient language lacked basic words, he starts a process of creating a dictionary for Modern Hebrew and establishes Va'ad HaLashon (the Language Committee, which later becomes the Academy of the Hebrew Language). Alongside other Hebrew grammarians and scholars, Eliezer starts teaching Hebrew in schools. In 1922, Hebrew gets recognized as the official language of the Jews living in Mandate Palestine. In 1948, the sacred language became the national language of the State of Israel.

SAY IT IN HEBREW / ARABIC

ENGLISH	HEBREW TRANSLITERATION	ARABIC TRANSLITERATION
English	Anglit	Ingleezi
Hello	shalom	mar-Ha-ba
Good morning	bo-ker tov	sa-baH el-kheir
Good evening	e-rev tov	masa el-kheir
Good night	lai-la tov	tes-ba-Hu Ala kheir
Thank you	to-da	shuk-run
You're welcome	al lo da-var	Af-wan
How are you?	ma shlom-kha?	keef Ha-lak?
	ma shlo-mekh?	keef Ha-lek?
What's up?	ma nish-ma?	shu el-akhbar?
What's going on?	ma ko-re?	shu sa-yer?
	ma ho-lekh?	keef el-'umoor?
	eikh ho-lekh?	keef ma-shi?
I'm fine	a-ni be-se-der	ta-mam
Nice to meet you	na-im me-od	etsharrafet bemA-reftak
		etsharrafet bemA-reftek
What's your name?	ma shim-kha? eikh ko-rim le-kha?	eish es-mak?
	ma shmekh? eikh ko-rim lakh?	eish es-mek?
My name is...	shmi... ko-rim li...	es-mi
Where are you from?	me-ei-fo a-ta?	Men wein en-tah?
	me-ei-fo at?	men wein en-ti
I'm from the US	a-ni me-ar-tsot ha-brit	ana men el-wi-lay-at el-mot-taHideh
Where do you live?	ei-fo a-ta gar?	wein sak-en?
	ei-fo at ga-ra?	wein sak-ne?
Congratulations	ma-zal tov.	mab-rook
"My love" (slang) in reference to a friend	ma-mi / ma-mush	ha-bibi
	ma-mi / ma-mush	ha-bib-ti
Let's go (slang)	yalla	yalla
Great! (slang)	sa-baba	sa-baba

THE LORD'S PRAYER HEBREW

Avinu shebashamayim, yitkadesh shimkha.
Tavo malkhutekha, ye'aseh r'tzonekha,
ba'aretz ka'asher na'asah vashamayim.
Ten-lanu haiyom lechem chukeinu.
U'selach lanu et-ashmateinu ka'asher
solchim anachnu la'asher ashmu lanu.
Ve'al-tevieinu lidei massah, ki im hatsileinu min-hara.
Ki lekha ha-mamlakha vehagevurah
veha-tiferet l'olanei olamim. Amen.

אָבִינוּ שֶׁבַּשָּׁמַיִם, יִתְקַדֵּשׁ שְׁמֶךָ,

תָּבוֹא מַלְכוּתֶךָ, יֵעָשֶׂה רְצוֹנְךָ כְּבַשָּׁמַיִם כֵּן בָּאָרֶץ.

אֶת לֶחֶם חֻקֵּנוּ תֶּן לָנוּ הַיּוֹם,

וּסְלַח לָנוּ עַל חֲטָאֵינוּ כְּפִי שֶׁסּוֹלְחִים גַּם אֲנַחְנוּ לַחוֹטְאִים לָנוּ.

וְאַל תְּבִיאֵנוּ לִידֵי נִסָּיוֹן, כִּי אִם חַלְּצֵנוּ מִן הָרָע.

כִּי לְךָ הַמַּמְלָכָה וְהַגְּבוּרָה וְהַתִּפְאֶרֶת לְעוֹלְמֵי עוֹלָמִים. אָמֵן.

THE LORD'S PRAYER ARABIC

Abana allathi fessamawat, liyataqaddas esmoka.
Liya'ti malakootuka, litakun mashy'atuka,
Kama fessama' kathalika Ala alard.
Chubzab kafafana aAtina elyawm
Waghfer lana thunubana kama naghfer naHnu 'aydan
lelmuthnibeena 'ilayna
Wala tudkhilna fe tajriba, laken najjina min ashirrir
Li'an laka almulka, walquwwa, walmajd, 'ila al'abad. Ameen.

أَبَانَا الَّذِي فِي السَّمَاوَات، لِيَتَقَدَّس اسْمُكَ.

لِيَأْت مَلَكُوتُكَ. لِتَكُنْ مَشِيئَتُكَ كَمَا فِي السَّمَاءِ كَذَلِكَ عَلَى الْأَرْضِ.

خُبْزَنَا كَفَافَنَا أَعْطِنَا الْيَوْمَ.

وَاغْفِرْ لَنَا ذُنُوبَنَا كَمَا نَغْفِرُ نَحْنُ أَيْضًا لِلْمُذْنِبِينَ إِلَيْنَا.

وَلَا تُدْخِلْنَا فِي تَجْرِبَة، لَكِنْ نَجِّنَا مِنَ الشِّرِّيرِ.

لِأَنَّ لَكَ الْمُلْكَ، وَالْقُوَّةَ، وَالْمَجْدَ، إِلَى الْأَبَدِ. آمِينَ.

163

ISRAEL FUN FACTS

- Hebrew is the only ancient language that has ever been successfully revived.

- Albert Einstein was offered the position of President of Israel, but he declined.

- Israel has more museums per capita than any other country.

- The world's first mobile phone, SMS messaging and AOL instant messaging were pioneered by Israelis.

- Israel is the only county to have more trees today than it did 50 years ago.

- Thanks to its national snack (Bamba), babies in Israel are 10 times less likely to suffer from peanut allergies.

- Coffee and cafés are so good in Israel that it's the only country where Starbucks failed trying to break into the local market.

- Israel is the only country in the Middle East where the number of Christians is increasing.

- Being on the junction of 3 continents, Israel has one of the highest concentrations of bird traffic in the world—500 million birds migrate across its airspace each year.

- Israel is only 1/6 of 1% of the landmass of the Middle East.

- Israel has the highest number of university degrees per capita than any other country.

- Israel has the world's highest rate of entrepreneurship among women.

- Israel's Dead Sea is the lowest place on earth and is 8.6 times saltier than the ocean.

- Israel is the first country to place a ban on the use of underweight models on catwalks.

- The Mount of Olives in Jerusalem is the world's oldest continuously used cemetery.

- Israelis who observe Shabbat can buy car insurance that doesn't cover Saturdays.

- By law, the Jewish National and University Library receives copies of every book printed in Israel.

- Israel's Save a Child's Heart organization performs life-saving heart operations for children worldwide, including many Palestinians, free of charge.

- Voicemail technology was developed in Israel.

- Life expectancy in Israel is among the highest in the world, at 82 years.

- The glue on Israeli stamps is kosher.

- Israeli banknotes have Braille on them to assist the blind.

Q. Who was the greatest female financier in the Bible?

A. Pharaoh's daughter -- she went down to the bank of the Nile and drew out a little profit. (Oops. That should read "prophet")

Q. Why was Goliath so surprised when David hit him with a slingshot?

A. The thought had never entered his head before.

Q. Why didn't Noah go fishing?

A. He only had two worms.

Q. Why couldn't Jonah trust the ocean?

A. Because he knew there was something fishy about it.

Q. Where was Solomon's temple located?

A. On the side of his head.

Q. Who was the fastest runner in the race?

A. Adam, because he was first in the human race.

Q. Which area of Palestine was especially wealthy?

A. The area around the River Jordan. The banks were always overflowing.

Q. What kind of man was Boaz before he married Ruth?

A. Absolutely ruthless.

Q. Who was the smartest man in the Bible?

A. Abraham. He knew a Lot.

Q. What's a dentist's favorite hymn?

A. Crown him with many crowns.

CROSSWORD PUZZLE (NT SITES)

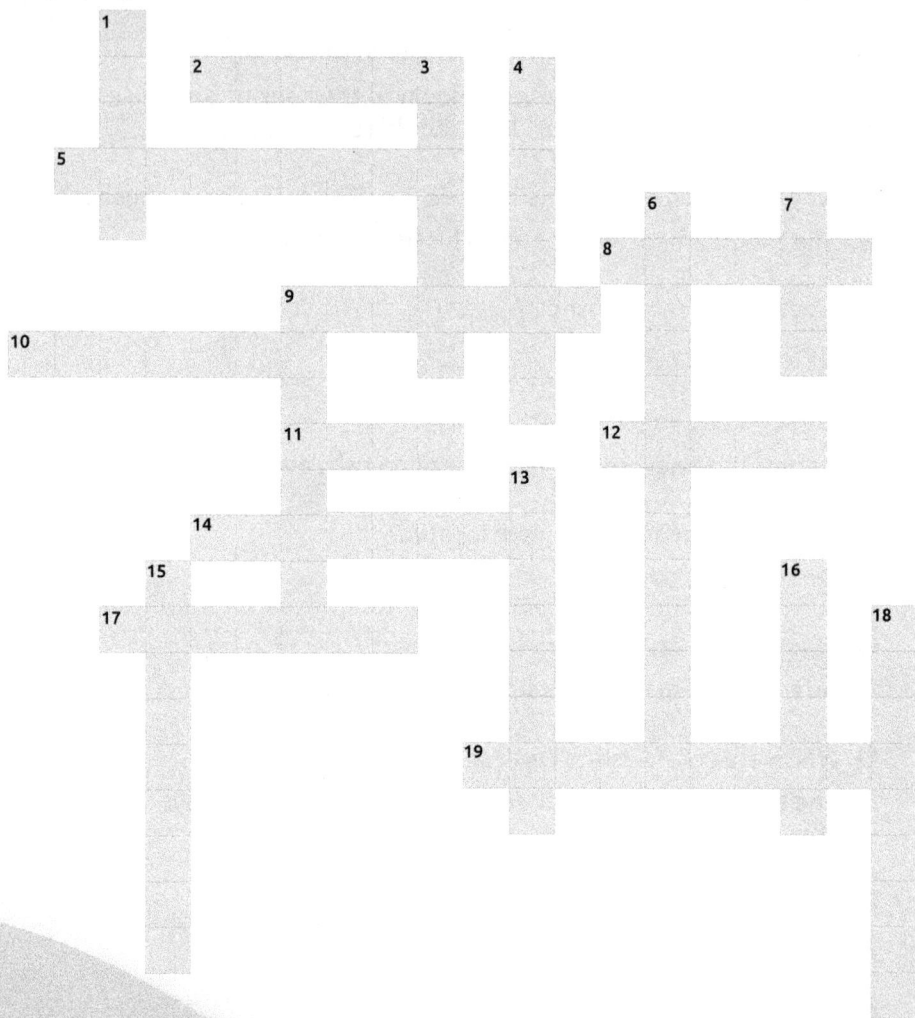

166

CLUES

ACROSS

2   Two disciples met the risen Christ on this road
5   City where Jesus was born
8   Jesus was baptized in this river
9   Jesus first met Peter and Andrew fishing in this Sea
10 Where Jesus met Zaccheus
11 Philip met an Ethiopian eunuch on this road
12 Dorcas, the kind and generous seamstress, was healed here
14 The pool in Jerusalem where a man lay for 38 years
17 Hometown of Mary, Martha and Lazarus
19 Jesus prayed in this garden shortly before his crucifixion

DOWN

1   Region containing Jerusalem and Bethlehem
3   Region between Judea and Galilee where Jesus traveled
4   Where Jesus lived as a child
6   The hill from which Jesus ascended to Heaven (3 words)
7   Where Jesus performed his first miracle
9   The "Place of a Skull," where Jesus was hung on the cross
13 City built by Herod the Great, home of Cornelius
15 City where Jesus made his triumphal entry
16 Samaritan city where Jesus met a woman at the well
18 City where the centurion's servant was healed from a distance

From - Km /(Miles)	Eilat	Be'er Sheva	Tiberias	Haifa	Tel Aviv	Jerusalem
Jerusalem	309 (193)	81 (50)	152 (95)	151 (94)	58 (36)	-
Tel Aviv	346 (220)	105 (65)	134 (83)	95 (59)	-	58 (36)
Haifa	438 (273)	197 (123)	69 (43)	-	95 (59)	151 (94)
Tiberias	405 (253)	233 (145)	-	69 (43)	134 (83)	152 (95)
Beer Sheba	241 (150)	-	233 (145)	197 (123)	105 (65)	81 (50)
Eilat	-	241 (150)	405 (253)	438 (273)	346 (120)	309 (193)
Ben-Gurion Airport	354 (221)	113 (70)	133 (83)	107 (66)	15 (9)	43 (26)
Arad	219 (136)	45 (28)	234 (146)	242 (151)	150 (93)	100 (62)
Ashdod	317 (198)	76 (47)	166 (100)	140 (87)	37 (23)	66 (41)
Ashkelon	307 (190)	66 (41)	183 (114)	157 (98)	54 (33)	71 (44)
Beit Shean	368 (230)	195 (121)	37 (23)	70 (43)	117 (73)	115 (71)
Beit Shemesh	333 (208)	92 (57)	169 (105)	136 (85)	42 (26)	27 (16)
Banias (Golan)	475 (296)	303 (189)	70 (43)	114 (71)	204 (127)	222 (138)
Herzliya	350 (218)	120 (75)	120 (75)	85 (53)	10 (6)	66 (41)
Jericho	289 (180)	163 (101)	116 (72)	149 (93)	97 (60)	36 (22)
Metula	469 (293)	297 (185)	64 (40)	120 (75)	198 (123)	216 (135)
Mitzpe Ramon	148 (92)	80 (50)	313 (195)	277 (173)	185 (115)	161 (100)
Nazareth	488 (305)	207 (129)	29 (18)	35 (21)	102 (63)	131 (81)
Netanya	372 (232)	131 (81)	101 (63)	66 (41)	29 (18)	85 (53)
Sdom (Dead Sea)	195 (121)	79 (49)	210 (131)	275 (171)	184 (115)	124 (77)

Abba: (Heb: *father*) An affectionate way to say Father in Hebrew.

Adonai: (Heb: *my Lord*) a Hebrew name for God signifying His sovereignty. It is also used as a representation of the unpronounceable tetragrammaton of YHVH (Yahweh).

Aelia Capitolina: The name given to pagan Jerusalem after its destruction by the Roman Emperor Hadrian in the Second Jewish Revolt (132-135 AD).

Aijalon Valley: Located in the Shephelah (low-lands) region, this is the valley where the sun stood still in the battle between Joshua and the five Amorite kings (*Josh 10:13*).

Aliyah: (Heb: *to go up*) The term used in reference to immigration to Israel.

Apocrypha: (Gre: *hidden, secret*) Ancient biblical literature than was not included in the original canonized Bible, such as the Maccabees, Judith, Tobit, Sirach, and others.

Aramaic: Semitic language spoken in the Babylonian, Persian, and Assyrian empires which is very similar to modern Hebrew and Arabic. Jesus spoke Aramaic and the language is somewhat still spoken today.

Armageddon: (Hebrew Transliteration from Har Megiddo: *Hill of Megiddo*), According to Revelation 16:16, the final battle between good and evil will take place here.

Ashkenazi: Term generally refers to Jews from Europe.

Baal: Canaanite god of fertility and often portrayed as the god of storms, lightning, thunder, and rain. He was worshipped in horrible ways. The name means "lord" or "master."

Balfour Declaration: Statement issued by the British Government in 1917 recognizing the Jewish people's right to a national home in the British Mandate of Palestine, named for British Foreign Secretary Arthur Balfour who signed it on Britain's behalf.

Bar Kokhba Revolt: The second Jewish revolt against Rome (132-135 AD) lead by the warrior Bar Kokhba and the prominent sage Rabbi Akiva.

Beelzebub: (Heb: *lord of the flies*) Name of the god of the Philistines. Term used by Jesus to refer to the prince of demons, the devil.

Beit Midrash: (Heb: *House of Study*) A place set aside for the study of sacred texts such as the Torah and the Talmud, generally a part of the synagogue or attached to it.

Byzantine Period: Established in 324 AD in the eastern part of the Roman Empire after the emperor Constantine adopted Christianity as the religion of the Roman Empire. Byzantine refers to Byzantium (Istanbul) which is where Constantine ruled from.

Canaan: The Old Testament name for the Promised Land. It means "land of purple," referring to the color of the dye produced from shellfish along Canaan's coast, primarily by the Phoenicians.

Canaanite: The people who lived in the land of Canaan. The term may have meant "merchant" or trader" as the trade route passed through this land.

Cardo: The main street in ancient Roman cities. It runs north to south and is lined with columns on both sides.

Chanukiah: a nine-branched menorah used during Hanukkah. One central candle provides the source of light for the eight other candles during the eight days of the celebration.

Coastal plain: the flat region running along the Mediterranean Sea. Most of Israel's population lives here.

Copper Scroll: One of the Dead Sea Scrolls, etched on copper, with a list of coded locations of ancient hidden treasure from before the destruction of the Second Temple.

Dead Sea Scrolls: Ancient Jewish manuscripts, including commentaries, instruction, and portions of most of the books of the Old Testament. They were discovered in 1947 near the Dead Sea in caves next to the ruins of Qumran.

Diaspora: Anywhere outside of Israel where Jewish people are settled.

Dome of the Rock: the shrine built in the seventh century on the holy sanctuary area commemorates the spot from which the Muslim prophet Mohammad traditionally ascended into heaven.

El Shaddai: (Heb: *God Almighty*) one of the names of the God of Israel.

Eretz Yisrael: (Heb: *The Land of Israel*) Territory of the ancient Israelite kingdom on both sides of the Jordan River, where the national and religious identity of the Jewish people was formed.

Firstfruits: The first part of the produce that belongs to God.

First Jewish Revolt / Great Revolt: Revolt against Rome by the Jewish people that resulted in the destruction of the Temple and Jerusalem in 70 AD.

Fresco: Design created by painting water colors on wet plaster.

Ghajar: An Alawite village located on the border of three nations: Syria, Lebanon, and Israel. With political complications during the war of 1967 leaving Ghajar in dire need of national sustainability, its residents requested to be occupied by Jewish State along with the Syrian Golan after Lebanon refused.

Great Rift Valley: Also known as the Jordan Valley, it is the valley east of Israel where the Sea of Galilee and the Dead Sea are located. It is the borderline between two tectonic plates which caused the deepest opening on earth.

Halacha: (Heb: *The Path*) Jewish law governing everyday life recorded and expounded upon in the Talmud.

Hallel: A selection comprising Psalms 113-118 and 135-136 chanted during Jewish feasts.

Har: Hebrew from "hill" or "mountain."

Hasmoneans: A Jewish priestly family who led the revolt against the Greeks who were establishing their own independent kingdom in the Land of Israel. Also known as the Maccabees.

HaShem: (Heb: *The Name*) Title used instead of saying God's name.

Hellenism: Greek civilization that spread through the ancient world from 333 BC. In Hellenistic culture, the human being is the ultimate reality, his mind the basis for truth, the body ultimate in wisdom, and pleasure the ultimate goal in life.

Hinnom / Gehenom: Valley to the west of Jerusalem which was the location of the child sacrifices to the god Molech. Because of the wickedness, ashes, rotten flesh, and the terrible smell of this valley, it came to symbolize hell. The Arabic word for hell "Jehennam" directly derives from the name of this valley.

Hippodrome: (Gre: *Horse Course*). An elongated race track used in the ancient world for horse races, chariot races, and Olympic-style games. In an attempt to Hellenize the land of Israel, Herod built hippodromes in Caesarea, Jericho, and Jerusalem.

Holocaust: (Gre: *Entire Burnt Offering*) a term used to refer to the genocidal Nazi policy of systematic industrial extermination of the Jewish people during World War II.

Jewish National Fund: Development fund founded in 1920 by the World Zionist Organization that purchased land from the Turks.

Jezreel Valley: Large, flat, fertile plain in northern Israel between the Galilee Mountains and the Samaria Mountains. The Via Maris passed through this area. The valley was also known as the Valley of Armageddon.

Josephus: Jewish general and author in the latter part of the 1st century AD who wrote *A History of the Jews* with a detailed account of the Jewish Revolt against Rome in 66-73 AD.

Judea: New Testament name for the Promised Land after the Babylonian Captivity (586 BC). Initially, it referred to the area that belonged to the tribe of Judah.

Judean Mountains: Also known as the Central Mountains, it is a region consisting of three mountain ranges Hebron in the south, Judea in the center, and Samaria in the north.

Judean Wilderness: The eastern slopes of the Judean Mountains which fall into the Great Rift Valley. Very little rain falls here, and so there are very few plants and animals.

Kabbalah: (Heb: *Receiving*) a system of Jewish theology and mysticism that developed in the 16th century.

Kibbutz: unique form of rural Jewish settlement based on the principle of joint property ownership and equality between all members.

Kidron Valley: Deep valley which was the eastern border of Jerusalem between the City of David and the Mount of Olives.

Kosher: Refers to food fit to be eaten according to Jewish law.

Legion: A military unit of 3,000-6,000 men in the ancient Roman army. Composed of spear mean, archers, strategists, cavalry, and reserves. Legion also was used to describe an army of angels or a host of demons.

Makhtesh: an erosion crater unique to the Middle East. There are three Makhteshim in the Negev.

Matzah: Unleavened flatbread, usually in the form of a large square cracker, which is eaten by Jews during Passover.

Menorah: a seven-branched candelabra.

Mezuzah: A parchment scroll with selected Torah verses placed in a container and affixed to the exterior doorpost of homes (*Deut 6:4-9; 11:13-21*).

Mikveh: A Jewish ritual bath for washing away spiritual impurity by immersion. There is a strong possibility that it is the background for baptism. A mikveh must be deep enough for full body immersion and with a volume of no less than 1 cubic meter. It was necessary that the water was "living water" to ensure purity; therefore, most of the water came from aqueducts from streams or rivers.

Mishnah: (Heb: *Repetition*) The written collection of the Jewish Oral Law as it existed at the end of the 2nd century.

Moab Mountains: a mountain range east of the Dead Sea where the Moabites lived (modern Jordan).

Moshav: A type of rural Jewish settlement where farms are individually but collectively worked and its produce shared by the community.

Moshe: (Heb: *Moses*) the prophet through whom the Torah was given to the people of Israel.

Mount Hermon: The highest mountain in Israel which is located on its northern border and is often covered with snow. Water from the melted snow flows down from the Hermon and creates the Jordan river.

Mount Sodom: Mountain ridge at the southern end of the Dead Sea which is composed almost entirely of salt. It retains the name of the city of Sodom, which was probably nearby.

Mount Sinai: The mountain where God gave Moses the 10 Commandments and established His covenant with the Israelites. Moses descended from Mount Sinai with a face so bright that he had to cover it.

Mount Tabor: A striking mountain at the northeastern edge of the Valley of Jezreel. It is also the site of the battle where Deborah and Barak defeated Jabin, king of Hazor.

Murex shellfish: Shellfish found along the coast of the Mediterranean Sea in northern Israel. Purple dye was produced with these shellfish, its production mainly associated with the Phoenicians.

Nazirite: Individual who showed his devotion to God by choosing to separate himself from other people through his lifestyle. He made a three-part vow: to abstain from any grape product, to never cut his hair or beard, and to avoid contact with anything dead. Samson was a Nazarite (*Num 6:1-21; Jdg 13:5,7; 16:17*).

Northern kingdom: After Solomon's death (926 BC), the kingdom of Israel was divided into two. The northern 10 tribes under Jeroboam became Israel. It was destroyed by the Assyrians in 722 BC.

Oral Law: Jewish belief that God reveals instructions for living through both the written Scripture and through a parallel process of orally transmitted traditions.

Ossuary: Depository for bones for second burial, common in the times of the New Testament.

Pentateuch: (Gre: *Five Books*) The first five books of the Bible: Genesis, Exodus, Leviticus, Numbers, and Deuteronomy. Also known as the Torah.

Peristyle garden: A Roman style garden inside a colonnaded area. Herod the Great built several peristyle gardens, including Jericho and Herodion.

Pilgrim Festivals: The three major festivals of Passover, Weeks, and Tabernacles in which every Jewish male was obligated to make a pilgrimage to Jerusalem to bring a sacrifice.

Procurator: Roman military governor. Pontius Pilate was procurator of Judea at the time of the crucifixion.

Rabbi: An authorized teacher/sage of the classical Jewish tradition. After the fall of the Second Temple in 70 AD, the role of the rabbi changed considerably.

Rabbinic Judaism: Jewish religious practice after the Temple was destroyed (AD 70) that centered around the Torah and its interpretation by the rabbis.

Rosh Hashana: (Heb: *Head of the Year*) A festival celebrated as the day God created Adam and Eve, the birthday of the universe.

Sabra: (Heb: *prickly cactus*)Term refers to Jews born in Israel.

Samaria Mountains: the northern mountain range of the central mountains in Israel. The Samaritans lived here.

Second Temple Period: Literally the period from the rebuilding of the Temple (516 BC) to its destruction by the Romans in 70 AD. The term usually refers to the latter part of the period beginning with the Hasmonean uprising in 168 BC and extending to the Bar Kokhba revolt in 135 AD.

Seder: (Heb: *order*) the Passover meal.

Sephardi: (Heb: *Spanish*) Term generally refers to Jews from the Mediterranean region.

Septuagint: (Latin: *70 / LXX*) The first Greek translation of the Old Testament (3rd-2nd century BC). It is named after the 70 translators.

Shalom: (Heb: *peace*) A Hebrew salutation coming from the rootword SHALEM meaning "wholeness, peace, tranquility, safety, prosperity."

Shema: (Heb: *Hear and Obey!*) Deuteronomy 6:4, the supreme affirmation of God's nature in Judaism.

Shephelah: the lowland region of Israel, between the coastal plain and the Judean mountains.

Shofar: An elaborate trumpet made of a ram's horn. The idea is linked to the ram caught in the thicket and sacrificed by Abraham in place of Isaac. The shofar was used to intimidate enemies, call people to assembly, and announce prayer times, the start and end of Sabbath, and holy days — e.g.Rosh Hashana, Yom Kippur, Succoth, and Passover. It is believed that this trumpet will signal the final judgment at the end of time.

Sinai Peninsula: Peninsula south of Israel where the Israelites wandered for 40 years.

Soreq Valley: Valley in the Shephelah where Samson lived.

Southern Kingdom: When Israel divided after Solomon's death (926 BC), the tribe of Judah under Rehoboam became the southern kingdom of Judah. In 586 BC, the Kingdom of Judah fell to the Babylonians under Nebuchadnezzar, and the Temple was destroyed.

Stele: A monumental standing stone with an inscription. Our modern practice of placing tombstones over the graves of loved ones probably derives from this.

Sukkoth: (Heb: *Tabernacles* or *Booths*) a week-long celebration of the Harvest Festival which commemorates God's protection and provision for Israel during 40 years in the desert.

Syncretism: the combining or attempted combining of different beliefs or practices, such as the gods Jupiter (Roman) and Zeus (Greek) believed to be one and the same. The Lord punished the Israelites when they practiced syncretism by trying to worship both God and Baal.

Synoptic Gospels: the name given to the first three Gospels in the New Testament (*Matthew, Mark, and Luke*), which view the story of Jesus from the same general perspective.

Tallit: the rectangular Jewish prayer shawl which has fringes (Tzitzit) on the four corners.

Talmud: (Heb: *Study*) A collection of Jewish writings comprising the Mishnah and Gemara. There are two Talmuds, the Babylonian and Jerusalem Talmud.

Tanakh: TaNaKh is an acronym of the traditional subdivisions of the books in the Hebrew Bible - Torah (*'Teaching'*, aka the first five books of Moses), Neviim (*'Prophets'*), and Ketuvim (*'Writings'*).

Tefillin/phylacteries: Leather boxes worn by the Jewish adult males on their arm and forehead. They contain scrolls of parchment with inscribed scriptures (*Exod 13:1-10, 11-16; Deut 6:4-9; 11:13-21*).

Tel: Large man-made mound or hill composed of layers of debris from several different periods of settlement.

Torah: (Heb: *instruction, guidance, teaching*) It refers to the first five books of Moses but can also refer to the entire Hebrew Bible and the Oral Law. Torah has also come to mean Jewish culture and teaching.

Valley of Jehoshaphat: (Heb: *Yahweh Has Judged*). The valley where all the people will be gathered on Judgement Day. Believed to be the valley of Kidron east of Jerusalem (*Joel 3:12*).

Wilderness of Paran: Wilderness just south of Israel in the Sinai Peninsula where the Israelites wandered for 40 years.

Yeshua: (Heb: *Salvation*) the Hebrew name for Jesus.

Yom Kippur: (Heb: *Day of Atonement*) an annual national day of fasting and prayer.

10,000 Reasons

Verse 1
The sun comes up, it's a new day
dawning
It's time to sing Your song again
Whatever may pass and whatever
lies before me
Let me be singing when the
evening comes

Chorus
Bless the Lord, O my soul, O my soul
Worship His holy name
Sing like never before, O my soul
I'll worship Your holy name

Verse 2
You're rich in love and You're slow
to anger
Your name is great and Your heart
is kind
For all Your goodness, I will keep
on singing
Ten thousand reasons for my
heart to find

Verse 3
And on that day when my strength
is failing
The end draws near and my time
has come
Still, my soul will sing Your praise
unending
Ten thousand years and then
forevermore

Amazing Grace

Verse 1
Amazing grace!
How sweet the sound
That saved a wretch like me!
I once was lost, but now am found;
Was blind, but now I see

Verse 2
Twas grace that taught my heart

to fear,
And grace my fears relieved;
How precious did that grace appear
The hour I first believed

Chorus
My chains are gone,
I've been set free
My God, my Savior has ransomed me
And like a flood His mercy reigns
Unending love,
Amazing grace

Verse 3
Through many dangers, toils, and
snares,
I have already come;
'Tis grace hath brought me safe
thus far,
And grace will lead me home

Verse 4
The Lord has promised good to me,
His Word my hope secures;
He will my Shield and Portion be,
As long as life endures

Verse 5
Yea, when this flesh and heart
shall fail,
And mortal life shall cease,
I shall possess, within the veil,
A life of joy and peace

Verse 6
The earth shall soon dissolve
like snow,
The sun forbear to shine;
But God, who called me here below,
Will be forever mine

Verse 7
When we've been there ten
thousand years,
Bright shining as the sun,
We've no less days
to sing God's praise
Than when we'd first begun

BE THOU MY VISION

Verse 1
Be Thou my Vision,
O Lord of my heart
Naught be all else to me,
save that Thou art
Thou my best Thought,
by day or by night
Waking or sleeping,
Thy presence my light

Verse 2
Be Thou my Wisdom,
and Thou my true Word
I ever with Thee and
Thou with me, Lord
Thou my great Father,
I Thy true son
Thou in me dwelling,
and I with Thee one

Verse 3
Riches I heed not,
nor man's empty praise
Thou mine Inheritance,
now and always
Thou and Thou only,
first in my heart
High King of Heaven,
my Treasure Thou art

Verse 4
High King of Heaven,
my victory won
May I reach Heaven's joys,
O bright Heav'n's Sun!
Heart of my own heart,
whate'er befall
Still be my Vision,
O Ruler of all

CORNERSTONE

Verse 1
My hope is built on nothing less
Than Jesus' blood and righteousness
I dare not trust the sweetest frame
But wholly trust in Jesus' name

Chorus
Christ alone; cornerstone
Weak made strong in the
Savior's love
Through the storm,
He is Lord
Lord of all

Verse 2
When Darkness seems
to hide His face
I rest on His unchanging grace
In every high and stormy gale
My anchor holds within the veil
My anchor holds within the veil

Interlude
He is Lord Lord of All

Verse 3
When He shall come
with trumpet sound
Oh, may I then in Him be found
Dressed in His righteousness alone
Faultless stand before the throne

GOOD GOOD FATHER

Verse 1
Oh, I've heard a thousand stories
Of what they think You're like
But I've heard the tender whisper
Of love in the dead of night
And You tell me that You're pleased
And that I'm never alone

Chorus
You're a Good Good Father
It's who You are (x3)
And I'm loved by You
It's who I am (x3)

Verse 2
Oh, and I've seen many searching
For answers far and wide
But I know we're all searching
For answers only You provide
'Cause You know just what we need
Before we say a word

Bridge
You are perfect in all of Your ways
Perfect in all of Your ways
You are perfect in all of Your ways
Perfect in all of Your ways
You are perfect in all of Your ways
to us

Verse 3
Oh, it's love so undeniable
I, I can hardly speak
Peace so unexplainable
I, I can hardly think
As you call me deeper still (x3)
Into love, love, love

GREAT ARE YOU LORD
Verse 1
You give life, You are love
You bring light to the darkness
You give hope, You restore
Every heart that is broken
Great are You, Lord

Chorus
It's Your breath in our lungs
So we pour out our praise
We pour out our praise
It's Your breath in our lungs
So we pour out our praise
To You only

Verse
All the earth will shout
Your praise
Our hearts will cry
These bones will sing
Great are You, Lord

HOLY SPIRIT
Verse 1
There is nothing worth more
That will ever come close
No thing can compare
You're our living hope
Your presence Lord

Verse 2
I've tasted and seen
Of the sweetest of love
When my heart becomes free
And my shame is undone

Interlude
Your presence Lord

Chorus
Holy spirit, You are welcome here
Come flood this place and fill the
atmosphere
Your glory, God,
is what our hearts long for
To be overcome
by Your presence, Lord

Bridge
Let us become more aware
of Your presence
Let us experience the glory
of Your goodness

HOSANNA
Verse 1
I see the King of glory
Coming on the clouds with fire
The whole earth shakes
The whole earth shakes

Verse 2
I see His love and mercy
Washing over all our sin
The people sing
The people sing

Chorus
Hosanna hosanna
Hosanna in the highest
Hosanna hosanna
Hosanna in the highest

Verse 3
I see a generation
Rising up to take their place
With selfless faith
With selfless faith

Verse 4
I see a near revival
Stirring as we pray and seek
We're on our knees
We're on our knees

Bridge
Heal my heart and make it clean
Open up my eyes
to the things unseen
Show me how to love like You
have loved me
Break my heart for
what breaks Yours
Everything I am
for Your kingdom's cause
As I walk from earth into eternity

How Deep the Father's Love

Verse 1
How deep the Father's love for us
How vast beyond all measure
That He should give His only Son
To make a wretch His treasure
How great the pain of searing loss
The Father turns His face away
As wounds which mar
the Chosen One
Bring many sons to glory

Verse 2
Behold the man upon a cross
My sin upon His shoulders
Ashamed, I hear my mocking voice
Call out among the scoffers
It was my sin that held Him there
Until it was accomplished
His dying breath has brought me life
I know that it is finished

Verse 3
I will not boast in anything
No gifts, no power, no wisdom
But I will boast in Jesus Christ
His death and resurrection
Why should I gain from His reward?
I cannot give an answer
But this I know with all my heart
His wounds have paid my ransom

How Great is Our God

Verse 1
The splendor of a king
Clothed in majesty
Let all the earth rejoice
All the earth rejoice
He wraps Himself in light
And darkness tries to hide
And trembles at His voice
Trembles at His voice

Chorus
How great is our God
Sing with me
How great is our God
And all will see
How great, how great is our God

Verse 2
Age to age He stands
And time is in His hands
Beginning and the end
Beginning and the end
The Godhead Three in One
Father, Spirit and Son
The Lion and the Lamb
The Lion and the Lamb

Bridge
Name above all names
Worthy of all praise
My heart will sing
How great is our God

In Christ Alone

Verse 1
In Christ alone my hope is found
He is my light, my strength,
my song
This Cornerstone, this solid Ground
Firm through the fiercest drought
and storm
What heights of love,
what depths of peace
When fears are stilled,
when strivings cease
My Comforter, my All in All
Here in the love of Christ I stand

Verse 2

In Christ alone! Who took on flesh
Fullness of God in helpless babe
This gift of love and righteousness
Scorned by the ones He came to save
Till on that cross as Jesus died
The wrath of God was satisfied
For every sin on Him was laid
Here in the death of Christ I live

Verse 3

There in the ground His body lay
Light of the world by darkness slain
Then bursting forth in glorious Day
Up from the grave He rose again
And as He stands in victory
Sin's curse has lost its grip on me
For I am His and He is mine
Bought with the precious blood of
Christ

Verse 4

No guilt in life, no fear in death
This is the power of Christ in me
From life's first cry to final breath
Jesus commands my destiny
No power of hell, no scheme of man
Can ever pluck me from His hand
Till He returns or calls me home
Here in the power of Christ I'll stand

LORD I NEED YOU

Verse 1
Lord, I come, I confess
Bowing here I find my rest
Without You I fall apart
You're the One that guides my heart

Chorus
Lord, I need You, oh, I need You
Every hour I need You
My one defence, my righteousness
Oh God, how I need You

Verse 2
Where sin runs deep
Your grace is more
Where grace is found
is where You are

Where You are, Lord, I am free
Holiness is Christ in me

Bridge
So teach my song to rise to You
When temptation comes my way
When i cannot stand I'll fall on You
Jesus, You're my hope and stay

MAN OF SORROWS

Verse 1
Man of sorrows Lamb of God
By His own betrayed
The sin of man and wrath of God
Has been on Jesus laid

Verse 2
Silent as He stood accused
Beaten mocked and scorned
Bowing to the Father's will
He took a crown of thorns

Chorus
Oh that rugged cross
My salvation
Where Your love
poured out over me
Now my soul cries out
Hallelujah
Praise and honour unto Thee

Verse 3
Sent of heaven God's own Son
To purchase and redeem
And reconcile the very ones
Who nailed Him to that tree

Bridge
Now my debt is paid
It is paid in full
By the precious blood
That my Jesus spilled
Now the curse of sin
Has no hold on me
Whom the Son sets free
Oh is free indeed

Verse 4
See the stone is rolled away
Behold the empty tomb

Hallelujah God be praised
He's risen from the grave

No Longer Slaves
Verse 1
You unravel me with a melody
You surround me with a song
Of deliverance from my enemies
'Til all my fears are gone

Chorus
I'm no longer a slave to fear
I am a child of God
I'm no longer a slave to fear
I am a child of God

Verse 2
From my mother's womb
You have chosen me
Love has called my name
I've been born again to a family
Your blood flows through my veins

Bridge
You split the sea
So I could walk right through it
My fears are drowned in perfect love
You rescued me
And I will stand and sing
I am a child of God

Oceans (Where Feet May Fail)
Verse 1
You call me out upon the waters
The great unknown
where feet may fail
And there I find You in the mystery
In oceans deep
My faith will stand

Chorus 1
And I will call upon Your name
And keep my eyes above the waves
When oceans rise
My soul will rest in Your embrace
For I am Yours and You are mine

Verse 2
Your grace abounds in deepest waters
Your sovereign hand
Will be my guide
Where feet may fail and fear
surrounds me
You've never failed and You won't
start now

Bridge
Spirit lead me where my trust is
without borders
Let me walk upon the waters
Wherever You would call me
Take me deeper than my feet
could ever wander
And my faith will be made stronger
In the presence of my Saviour

Chorus 2
I will call upon Your name
Keep my eyes above the waves
My soul will rest in Your embrace
I am Yours and You are mine

What a Beautiful Name
Verse 1
You were the Word at the beginning
The One with God
the Lord Most High
Your hidden glory in creation
Now revealed in You, our Christ

Chorus
What a beautiful name it is
What a beautiful name it is
The name of Jesus Christ, my King
What a beautiful name it is
Nothing compares to this
What a beautiful name it is
The Name of Jesus, Jesus

Verse 2
You didn't want heaven without us
So Jesus, You brought heaven down
My sin was great, Your love was
greater
What could separate us now

What a wonderful Name it is
What a wonderful Name it is
The Name of Jesus Christ my King
What a wonderful Name it is
Nothing compares to this
What a wonderful Name it is
The Name of Jesus
What a wonderful Name it is
The Name of Jesus

Bridge
Death could not hold You, the veil
tore before You
You silenced the boast
of sin and grave
The heavens are roaring
the praise of Your glory
For You are raised to life again
You have no rival, You have no equal
Now and forever, God, You reign
Yours is the Kingdom,
Yours is the glory
Yours is the Name above all names

Chorus 3
What a powerful Name it is
What a powerful Name it is
The Name of Jesus Christ my King
What a powerful Name it is
Nothing can stand against
What a powerful Name it is
The Name of Jesus

WHAT TO SEE ON YOUR FREE DAY

(Please check with your guide first as you may have visited some of these sites already. Please call ahead to verify hours and fees as there may be group discounts).

TEMPLE INSTITUTE

Misgav Ladach St 40, Jerusalem

See and understand the story of the Holy Temple

(*Sunday to Thursday 9:00-17:00, Friday 9:00-14:00. Closed on Saturday*)

Entrance Fee: Adult 25 ILS, Guide, additional 70 ILS. (Group discounts available)

Tel: 02-6264545

CHRIST CHURCH COFFEE SHOP

Jaffa Gate across Tower of David Museum.

(*Open daily 9:00-20:00, Sundays 9:00-16:00*)

Tel: 02-6277727

ROCKEFELLER ARCHEOLOGICAL MUSEUM

Sultan Suleiman St 27, Jerusalem

This museum houses a large number of artifacts from excavations taking place during the British Mandate.

(*Sunday, Monday, Wednesday and Thursday 10:00 to 15:00; Saturday and Holidays 10:00 to 14:00; closed Tuesday and Friday*)

No Entrance Fee

Tel: 02-6282251

TOWER OF DAVID MUSEUM

Jaffa Gate 9114001, Jerusalem

This museum tells the story of the 4000 year old Jerusalem. Be sure to look out for the incredible Night Show events!

(*Open Daily: 9:00-16:00/17:00, Saturday 9:00-14:00*)

Entrance Fee: Adult 40 ILS

Tel: 02-6265333

RAMPART WALK

Paul Emile Botta St 5, Jerusalem

Walk along the walls of Jerusalem overlooking the beautiful city.

(*Open daily: 9:00-16:00, Fridays 9:00-14:00*)

Entrance Fee: Adult 16 ILS

Tel: 02-6277550

THE ISRAEL MUSEUM

Derech Ruppin 11, Jerusalem

Check out the wonderful exhibits and the Shrine of the Book (Dead Sea Scrolls).

(*Open Daily: Sunday, Monday, Wednesday, Thursday 10:00-17:00, Tuesday 16:00-21:00, Friday 10:00-14:00, Saturday 10:30-16:00*)

Entrance Fee: Adult 54 ILS

Tel: 02-6708888

Bible Lands Museum

Shmuel Stephan Weiz St 21

Explore the different cultures of the ancient peoples of the Bible.

(Open Monday, Tuesday, Thursday 9:30-17:30, Wednesday 9:30-21:30, Friday 10:00-14:00, closed on Sunday and Saturday)

Entrance Fee: Adult 44 ILS

Tel: 02-5611066

Yad Vashem Memorial Museum

Har Hazikaron (Mt. Remembrance)

Visit the beautiful yet tragic memorial for the Holocaust victims.

(Open Monday, Tuesday, Wednesday 8:30-17:00, Thursday 8:30-20:00, Friday 8:30-14:00, closed on Saturday and Sunday)

No Entrance Fee

Tel: 02-6443400

The Burnt House

2 Tiferet Israel St, Jerusalem

Visit the magnificent remains of a burnt house from the time of the destruction of the Second Temple and the upper part of Jerusalem.

(Opens Sunday to Thursday 9:00-19:00, Friday 9:00-1:00, closed on Saturday)

Entrance Fee: Adult 25 ILS

Tel: 02-6287211

City of David

Ma'alot Ir David St, Jerusalem

Visit the place where it all began! Journey back to the time when King David conquered and made Jerusalem his capital and enjoy the walk through Hezekiah's tunnel.

(Open Sunday to Friday 8:00-17:00, closed on Saturday)

Entrance Fee: Adult 65 ILS

Tel: 02-6268700

Yemin Moshe Neighborhood and Montefiore's Windmill

Walk through the picture perfect neighborhood which was established due to the overcrowding within the Old City itself.

Haas Promenade

Daniel Yanofsky Street

Enjoy a spectacular panoramic view of Jerusalem!

Jerusalem Biblical Zoo & Aquarium

Derech Aharon Shulov 1

Stroll through the beautiful park with over 170 diverse species of Biblical and endangered animals.

(Open everyday: Sunday through Thursday 9:00-19:00, Friday 9:00-16:30, Saturday 10:00-18:00)

Entrance Fee: Adult/Child 40 ILS

Tel: 02-6750111

FIRST TRAIN STATION

David Remez St 4, Jerusalem

Enjoy the vibrant atmosphere at the site of the Old Train Station anytime any day of the week.

(Open: *24/7*)

Tel: 02-6535239

ALLIANCE CHURCH

Al Rusul St 14, Old City of Jerusalem

Worship with the local Arab believers in the heart of Old City Jerusalem.

(Service: *Sunday 10:30*)

Tel: 02-6260711

KING OF KINGS

Jaffa St 97

Visit the English Messianic Congregation in the city center of Jerusalem.

(Service: *Sunday 17:00*)

Tel: 02-6251899

CHRIST CHURCH

Jaffa Gate

The oldest Protestant Church in the Middle East, instrumental in the return of the Jewish people to Israel.

(Services: *Sunday 9:30 and 19:00*)

Tel: 02-6277727

NAZARENE CHURCH IN NAZARETH

Paulus VI St, Nazareth

Worship with the local Arab Christians in Nazareth.

(Service: *Friday* 18:30, *Sunday* 10:00)

Tel: 04-6553062

ST. ANDREW'S TIBERIAS, THE CHURCH OF SCOTLAND

Gdud Barak St 1, Tiberias

Visit the ecumenical English-speaking church in the heart of the ancient city of Tiberias by the Sea of Galilee.

(Service: *Sunday 10:00*)

Tel: 054-2446736

Building a foundation will help orientate your group to the geographical, cultural and historical context of the land of the Bible, and will help tour participants get the most out of their trip. Below are some resources we recommend that can either be studied as a group or individually:

FILM: *The Jerusalem Film* – an IMAX film by National Geographic

DVD: *That The World May Know: Faith Lessons* - Ray Vander Laan

BOOK: *The Israelis: Ordinary People in an Extraordinary Land* - Dana Rosenfeld

BOOK: *Jesus Through Middle Eastern Eyes: Cultural Studies in the Gospels* - Kenneth E. Bailey

BOOK: *Our Father Abraham: Jewish Roots of the Christian Faith* - Marvin R. Wilson

BOOK: *One Friday in Jerusalem* - Andre Moubarak . (Website to order: *www.onefridayinjerusalem.com/shop*)

BOOK: *The Lemon Tree: An Arab, a Jew, and the Heart of the Middle East* - Sandy Tolan

BOOK: *Blood Brothers: The Unforgettable Story of a Palestinian Christian working for Peace in Israel* - Elias Chacour

WEBSITE: *www.antiquities.org.il* - Israel Antiquities Authority

WEBSITE: *www.akhlah.com/hebrew/worksheets/* - Jewish learning materials - try the alphabet lesson worksheets!

* The photographs in this book come from the collections available for Bible study and teachings at *bibleplaces.com* and *seetheholyland.net* *

TWINS TOURS & TRAVEL LTD

Twins Tours & Travel LTD.
Jaffa Rd. 97, Clal Building
Floor C2, Office #201
P.O. Box 28314
Jerusalem 91283
Israel

Office Phone: +972 2-579-8159
Mobile: +972 54-523-1145
USA: +1(512) 222-3160
Fax: +972 2-579-8158
Skype: twinstours

E-mail: info@twinstours.com

Websites: http://www.twinstours.org
http://www.onefridayinjerusalem.com
htttp://www.andremoubarak.com

Follow us: http://twitter.com/twinstours
Subscribe: http://plus.google.com/+twinstours
Circle Us: http://plus.google.com/+twinstours
Facebook:http://www.facebook.com/andre.moubarak
Instagram:http://instagram.com/twinstours

TRIP EVALUATION

We hope that you had a pleasant stay in the Holy Land, and we thank you for choosing our company for your travel arrangements. We would be grateful if you could take a moment to complete this questionnaire and return it to our representative in the supplied envelope at the end of your tour.

YOUR NAME:

GROUP NAME:

GUIDE'S NAME:

DRIVER'S NAME:

TRAVEL DATES:

Airport Assistance

    1   2   3   4   5   6   7   8   9   10

Accommodations

    1   2   3   4   5   6   7   8   9   10

Accompanying Guide

    1   2   3   4   5   6   7   8   9   10

Accompanying Driver

    1   2   3   4   5   6   7   8   9   10

Transportation

    1   2   3   4   5   6   7   8   9   10

Overall impression of your tour

    1   2   3   4   5   6   7   8   9   10

Comments:

If you would like to receive our newsletters and stay updated with what the Lord is doing in the Holy Land, please provide us with your contact information:

NAME:_____**PHONE:**_____

ADDRESS:_____

CITY:_____**STATE:**_____**ZIP:**_____

E-MAIL:_____

Your generous donations help Twins Tours to keep going and moving forward. Your gifts help us to create content, write articles, produce audio and video teachings, online classes, study tours, and so much more.

Partner with us today and help our teachings reach more places around the world while witnessing your gifts multiply. Visit our website to see how you can help spread the word of God through your donations:

TWINSTOURS.ORG/ BECOMEAPARTNER

Stay connected with Twins Tours via e-mail in order to receive our newsletters and stay updated with what the Lord is doing in the Holy Land.

Email: info@twinstours.com

Connect with Andre's personal number for videos and updates on WhatsApp: +972 54-523-1145

BLESSINGS FROM ISRAEL

www.ingramcontent.com/pod-product-compliance
Lightning Source LLC
Chambersburg PA
CBHW021954090426
42811CB00001B/20